I'M LISTENING AS FAST AS I CAN

The Night Ministry in San Francisco

I'M LISTENING AS FAST AS I CAN

The Night Ministry in San Francisco

DONALD E. STUART

50TH ANNIVERSARY EDITION
Commemorating 50 Years of the
San Francisco Night Ministry
1964 to 2014

San Francisco Night Ministry
San Francisco, California

ISBN 978-0-9907078-1-3

Editor: Sandra Gary

Book and cover design by Barbara Geisler Design

Cover photo by Patrick Boury [www.flickr.com/photos/pbo31]

Anniversary edition writing contributed by Sandra Gary,
Lyle J. Beckman, Charles H. Lewis, and Donald A. Fox

Copy editing by Donald A. Fox

Proofreading by Jessica Metoyer

Photography by Tom Jelick

Anniversary edition photography contributed by
Thomas Mikkelsen, Jock McDonald, Bryant Ward, and Bill Wasson

SAN FRANCISCO
NIGHT MINISTRY
50 YEAR ANNIVERSARY 1964-2014

San Francisco Night Ministry
1031 Franklin Street
San Francisco, CA 94109
www.sfnightministry.org

Printed in the United States of America

Contents

Foreword

Donald E. Stuart's book *I'm Listening as Fast as I Can* has touched the hearts of many since it was first published in 2003, and the Night Ministry is pleased to make this edition available, marking the 50th Anniversary of the Night Ministry in San Francisco. This book offers a vivid and valuable glimpse into the nightlife of San Francisco in the 1960s and 1970s and of the "people of the night." In story after story, Don Stuart shows how he and the Night Ministry staff and volunteers responded to those who were facing difficult trials or crises in their lives. This book also connects us to our roots, and shows the power of community, compassion and hope.

In some ways our ministry has not changed over time. Fifty years after its founding, the Night Ministry is still unique and continues to meet the human and spiritual needs of people facing loneliness, fear, despair, and confusion as they wrestle with the overwhelming questions and circumstances of life. Every night of the year, volunteer Crisis Line Counselors are on the phones and ordained clergy are on our streets, all dispensing compassion and understanding; offering counseling and referrals to anyone in need, in the middle of the night. This is still a ministry that is as urgently needed as it is challenging.

In other ways, the Night Ministry has been able to respond to the ever changing backdrop of cultural, political, economic and other factors that have helped make San Francisco what it is today. From the AIDS Crisis and earthquakes, to poverty, mental health, and housing issues, the Night Ministry continues to serve as the bridge that supports people, connecting them to daytime resources and services, and to the light that shines in the darkness of the night.

This 50th Anniversary edition of *I'm Listening as Fast as I Can* not only honors the early history and work of the Night Ministry, but gives us focus and direction as we move into the future with confidence and hope that those who need a place to turn to in the middle of the night will find us. Added to this edition are profiles of the four Night Ministers at the helm since the beginning; information about current Night Ministry programs including our vision for the years to come; and a timeline highlighting historical events in the Night Ministry's work since Donald Stuart's time.

Most importantly, this book honors the memory and ministry of Donald Stuart, who died peacefully at the age of 91 surrounded by family on March 5, 2014. For his service to the Church at large; for his compassion toward the most vulnerable among us; and for his vision for the Night Ministry which still lives on, I will be ever grateful. May your reading of this book help you to appreciate the enduring nature of Donald Stuart's work and inspire you in your own life of service to others.

Lyle J. Beckman
Director
San Francisco Night Ministry
July 2014

ACKNOWLEDGEMENTS

When the San Francisco Night Ministry Governing Board established a committee to mark our 50th anniversary, the first idea that took hold was to print an anniversary edition of Don Stuart's book *I'm Listening as Fast as I Can*. The Board's compassion for those whom we serve, their leadership in building a strong and vital ministry in San Francisco, and their vision for the future have served us well, especially in the efforts leading up to our anniversary celebration. Special thanks to Ron King, President; Charles Jacobs, Vice President; Dr. Elizabeth Lewis, Secretary; Larry Dannenberg, Treasurer; and to Board members Marian Brischle, Barry Clagett, the Rev. Eric Metoyer, Roy Mosley, Brother Tikhon Pethoud, Mary Van Zomeren, and Kathryn Wagner for their encouragement and support on this book project.

The 50th Anniversary Committee has taken on all of the many roles that you can expect when a significant anniversary is celebrated, from planning special events, to arranging for publicity, and rounding up the resources needed to accomplish it all. This book is one of several of their projects. I am grateful for their attention to detail and dedication to finding a way to tell our 50-year-long story. Special thanks to Co-Chairs Joanne Chadwick, who was Night Ministry's first coordinator of Crisis Line Counselors, and Dr. Rod Dugliss, who is the Dean of the Episcopal School for Deacons; and to our committee members: the Rev. Donald Fox, Sandra Gary, Ron King, Lorna Hill, the Rev. Dr. Sandra Hulse, the Rev. Charles Lewis, Bruce Pettit, and Rose Marie Springer.

Thanks to the current Night Ministry staffers who continue to help shape and sustain our ministry as they offer themselves in service, working faithfully under unusual and sometimes dangerous circumstances: Associate Night Ministers the Rev. Thom Longino and the Rev. Monique Ortiz; Coordinator of Crisis Line Counselors Brother Jude Hill; and our Assistant Night Ministers: the Rev. Adam Briones, the Rev. Donald Fox, the Rev. Berni Fricke, Br. Jude Hill, the Rev. Valerie McEntee, the Rev. Andreas Pielhoop, the Rev. Megan

Rohrer, the Rev. David Stickley, and the Rev. Diana Wheeler. Special thanks to our 45 Crisis Line Counselors, nameless here to protect confidentiality, for their skill in listening and their compassionate responses on the phone. The positive impact they have on the lives of thousands of people each year make them equally as important as our Governing Board and our paid staff.

Our support staff has been invaluable: Office Manager Jun Ranches, Night Ministry Associate Bruce Pettit, and Daytime Volunteer Coordinator Marilyn Shipp. Thanks also to Clinical Pastoral Education Supervisor the Rev. Rod Seeger, and to our Open Cathedral deacons and volunteers, especially the Rev. Vicki Gray, the Rev. Nancy Pennekamp, the Rev. Marcus Crim, the Rev. Ivan Casteñeda, and David Chew, Head Usher.

I am most grateful to Chuck Lewis and Don Fox. They are friends and mentors who have enthusiastically and lovingly introduced me to a ministry that has become as dear to my heart as it is to theirs. They continue to work tirelessly on the Night Ministry's behalf, and have contributed much of the information you see in this anniversary edition. For their witness, compassion, knowledge, humor, and friendship, I will always be grateful.

In addition, I am grateful to the Rev. Mark Stuart and Kathy Stuart Boyer, Don Stuart's children, who made it possible for us to reprint their father's book. Their blessing on this book project will never be forgotten.

Many people have worked diligently to make the words before you appear. Special thanks go to Sandra Gary for her excellent guidance, skill in turning a phrase, and countless hours spent as our editor, contributing writer, and project manager. Thanks, too, to book designer Barbara Geisler for her outstanding skills at layout and her knowledgeable advice on many aspects of making a book. We are grateful to photographer Patrick Boury for donating our cover photograph. Our gratitude also goes to graphic designer Thomas Mikkelsen for creating our logo and the medallion on the cover, and for contributing many photographs. Thanks, also, to Joey Plaster whose engaging audio histories have provided lively stories.

Finally, it is the people whom we serve, the people of the night, who also deserve our gratitude. They have received what the Night Ministry offers with appreciation and grace, and have blessed us by teaching us, trusting us, and making us better at what we do each night. To them we promise to always listen as fast as we can.

Lyle J. Beckman

Preface

I t is said that pain is not long remembered and the distasteful soon forgotten. I am not certain I believe that to be valid and true for all situations. It surely does not apply to the years I spent as Director of the Night Ministry from 1964 to 1976.

Although I retired from the Night Ministry more than twenty years ago, some of the experiences are just as vivid and just as painful as they were during the nights on which they occurred. I wonder whether I would have been so eager to accept the position if I could have foreseen just how traumatic many of the experiences would be. Yet, in retrospect, I can say, without equivocation, that I would do it all over again, and can affirm that my years in the Night Ministry were the richest and most rewarding years of my entire ministry.

I have often been asked why I had not written a book about my years on the street. Actually, I had written it, not only in my nightly journal and quarterly reports, but also in my mind and certainly in my heart. Nevertheless, as I gathered material for this book, I had to struggle to dredge up some memories of events long since passed and long since experienced. I found myself surprised by how deeply I had buried situations that I once thought I could never forget. I was also surprised by how many wounds still remain unhealed. I find it therapeutic in some ways to touch these wounds once more so that I can find the healing brought on by new experiences, new perspectives, and new growth—and especially by sharing.

Was the fact that I did not apply for the position, but instead, a third party had submitted my name as a candidate, indicative of "divine intervention?" For me it validated the fact that I was called by some force outside myself by what Carl Jung called, "a synchronous series of events." I soon discovered that developing a new ministry without precedent was both challenging and frightening. It was the sense of having been called coupled with the challenge of the unexpected that kept this Ministry fresh and challenging for me each night. I was walking where the traditional Church seldom walked, speaking to people usually ignored by both the traditional Church and by the "respectable" world. I was reaching beyond the structures of the institution and embracing those members of society who were most difficult to accept. The task encompassed all of my emotions and sometimes sapped my patience.

One of the major reasons for my being called to organize and develop the Night Ministry was that I had a track record in pastoral counseling with an understanding of the message of Jesus and a grasp of His non-judgmental acceptance of people. The Church of my youth taught me that we couldn't appreciate the total meaning of what it is to be human without including the Divine dimension. Without that Divine dimension, the essential difference between the human and the animal disappears. We are all children of the same God.

I believe that one of the major reasons so many of the people with whom I worked at night had difficulty in improving their life, or even in finding it, was the low opinion they held of themselves as well. They held so low a view of humanity that they had no incentive or saw no reason to lift or improve their own life-style. So many had difficulty in recognizing who they were not only in relationship to God, to their brothers and sisters, but especially to who they were within themselves.

It was not my objective to "preach" to street people in the usual sense. This was a ministry of presence, and presence at a time inconvenient for the traditional Church to respond. It was stemming the flow of blood from slashed wrists or from a beating. It was sharing the "Good News" through being there when no one else was, and at any time of the night. I rarely intruded on a person's privacy unless they gave me an opening to do so or unless my help was obviously needed. I didn't mark the success of my nights by counting up how many souls I had "saved" or how many new members I had added to the church rolls. I simply planted seeds. If my people couldn't see that the love of God was being shared with them through a tired and soaking-wet clergyman coming at two or three o'clock on a rainy morning, they would hardly hear my words.

A story (probably apocryphal) about St. Francis of Assisi was a constant inspiration to me and to the Night Ministry especially on a night when I thought nothing was happening: St. Francis invited a young novice to accompany him on a preaching expedition through the town. They passed through one street after another and eventually returned to their starting point without having spoken a word.

The novice said, "I thought we were going to preach."

"We have preached," replied St. Francis. "We were observed as we walked; the people saw us on the streets. That was how we preached."

Early in this ministry one of the first calls I received from the bus depot was from a security guard who asked me to help an elderly distraught woman suffering from dementia. When I met her in the dispatcher's office she began weeping and hysterically cried, "Who am I? Please tell me who I am." This was the cry I heard almost nightly from old and young alike, sometimes articulated but mostly implied. "Please tell me who I am."

In March of 1964, I wrote a letter to the Night Ministry Personnel Committee quoting from *Guilt* by Caryll Houselander. I agreed with this paragraph then, and after years of experience with the Night ministry I am even more convinced of its validity:

"It is time that Christians put aside their self-protective type of religion with its interminable formalities and careful exclusions and respectable cliques and recognize Christ and themselves in the disreputable members of the

Church, the socially ostracized; the repulsive, the criminals, the insane, the drifting population of the man or woman waiting in the condemned cell to die—and the tiresome, thankless members of a man or woman's own household. It is time that Christians answered Cain's question, 'Am I my brother's (or sister's) keeper' with more than an affirmative: I am more than that—I am my brother and my sister."

Donald E. Stuart
Claremont, California
September 2003

Mark Stuart, Jo Chadwick, and Chuck Lewis making merry in the early 1970s.

ACKNOWLEDGEMENTS

Many worked with the San Francisco Council of Churches to make the Night Ministry a possibility: Jack Smith, Executive Director of the Council; Bill Grace, Urban Director for the Presbyterian Church; Bill Black, Urban Director of the Lutheran Church in America; and Doug Siden, Urban Director of the American Baptist Church were some of the key persons who dreamed the dream into reality.

Two people who gave invaluable service to the Night Ministry, not only during its developmental stage, but also all during my twelve years on the job, were Chuck Lewis, Lutheran Church of America Pastor and organizer of his denomination's North Beach Fellowship, and Joanne Chadwick, a Lutheran Church in America Christian Education Director and Social Worker also associated with the same mission.

I began my work officially on September 1st, 1964, and on November 4th, 1964, Chuck was hired by the Night Ministry Board to be my associate. He would work one night a week and fill in during my vacation period. Soon after that, James Christiansen, a seminarian from PLTS in Berkeley joined Chuck to give me two nights a week off. When I retired in June 1976, the Night Ministry Board named Chuck to replace me as the full time Night Minister.

Chuck and Jo were not only my part time associates, but also my full time friends. Both Chuck and Jo were my support team, my confidants and my good friends through the years.

Sunday nights at Chuck's apartment in North Beach were "open house" to seminarians and often street people we had met during the week. Observers from the participating denominations and often people from other cities contemplating a night ministry program looked to us as a role model to see how to begin a similar program in their home city.

Within a short time after our street work began, we knew we would need volunteers. Jo was a natural to coordinate that project. She recruited volunteers from all walks of life: men and women, gay and straight. Some were from wealthy suburbs, some from communes, some from churches, some un-churched. No matter who they were, if they were willing to serve, they were recruited. She provided a training program and made them capable and sensitive counselors who were able to handle the myriad calls that came into the Night Ministry office.

The original participating denominations not only supported the Night Ministry with funds, but also each supplied a member to serve on the Board. They were: the American Baptist Convention, The Episcopal Church, the Lutheran Church in America, the Lutheran Church—Missouri Synod, the United Methodist Church, the United Church of Christ, and the United Presbyterian Church in the USA. Also of great help were the YMCA, the Salvation Army, and the Travelers Aid Society, who supplied rooms for the stranded. "Dutch" Hornstra, the manager of the Turk Street YMCA, was of tremendous help and support during my years with the Ministry. Financial support came not only from these seven denominational head-quarters, but also from innumerable congregations around the country, as well as from individuals who read about the Night Ministry in denomina-tional magazines or in press releases.

Dr. Richard Norberg, Conference Minister of the Northern California/ Nevada Conference of the United Church of Christ, under whose jurisdiction I worked, was always there for me. He knew my dreadful schedule and an-swered my calls when I needed him. He had given word to his staff that, even though he might be in a meeting, he was to be interrupted if I called. He was my Pastor during those years when my life and schedule were upside-down.

I owe a tremendous debt of thanks to my dear friend of many years and computer mentor, Corinne Bergmann, who patiently coached me, edited, and walked me through many problems and glitches that I would not have been able to solve on my own. Without her, this document in its present form would not have been possible. She also suggested, encouraged and prodded me into writing this story. She has looked over my shoulder offering suggestions and support when my muse was sleeping.

Not enough can be said about the help and support given by the writers' group offered at the Borders book store. They were sometimes hard task-masters, but always encouraging.

My children, Mark and Kathy, who were teenagers when I began my work in the Night Ministry, also deserve my thanks. It was not easy living with a father who slept when they were awake, and having to be quiet when their friends were visiting; or to have a father who couldn't go to evening school events or social gatherings without having to leave early to get to work. They didn't always understand, but they did always love.

But my greatest debt of gratitude goes to my wife Eunice, who moved to San Francisco reluctantly but supported me fully and lovingly. Many times when tragedy after tragedy pulled me down into my own "slough of despond," she was there to lift me up, encourage me, embrace me in her arms and allow me to weep myself clean of the pain I was trying to carry for others. Without her strength and support I could not have made it!

Donald E. Stuart

The San Francisco Night Ministry's first logo, designed by Don Stuart

Don listening as fast as he could.

CHAPTER 1

Beginnings

August. The last major influx of tourists wandered the streets seeking that elusive "San Francisco Experience." Still prevalent at this time of the year, the mountain-high fog-bank rolled through the Golden Gate in the afternoon, obliterating the bridge, creeping over Twin Peaks, blurring everything in its path. Soon the City was covered by a huge white blanket. The air was damp and chilly, the action hot and steamy.

I stood on the corner of Eddy and Taylor streets. The neon hands of the clock on the Budweiser sign in the liquor store across the street told me it was 11:30 p.m. Judging by the number of people milling about, it could have been the middle of the afternoon. This corner was the "Times Square" of illicit activity in the center of the Tenderloin district. This was where the action was. Whatever you wanted could be found within the toss of a beer bottle from where I stood. I had spent some days scouting out this area as a possible part of the City in which to begin my work, but tonight I was bombarded by sights and smells and feelings I had not experienced for many years. Twenty years ago as a young sailor stationed at the Naval Base on Treasure Island in the middle of San Francisco Bay, I frequented these same streets. I saw them now through older eyes, motivated by a different agenda.

A flood of thoughts surged through my mind. Some were second thoughts. Was this really where I belonged? Where I wanted to belong? Was this where I wanted to use my training and experience? What was I—an innocent, naive young clergyman from the Midwest—doing on a street like this in the middle of the night? Who and what were these people anyway? My lifestyle and experience was diametrically opposed to theirs. Would these "night people" accept me? Would there ever be any communication between us, or were we too many worlds apart? Would they ignore me, or worse, laugh me off the street? Within my mind, doubt and excitement whirled in a kind of frenzied dance.

I was forty-two years old. My last parish was in Lincoln, Nebraska. Now I was the newly designated San Francisco Night Minister.

My thoughts went back to my first parish in Nickerson, Kansas, a town of a thousand people in the center of the state. My wife Eunice and I, with our two children, Mark and Kathy, lived in town; our church was in the middle of a wheat field seven miles to the north. After six years in Nickerson, the United Church of Christ Board for Homeland Ministries called me to Lincoln, Nebraska, to develop a congregation in the growing south edge of the city. I thought now of the upwardly mobile young couples in Lincoln who were just starting their careers and families. How different they were from those with whom I would be working on the streets of San Francisco.

How had all this come about? In the early part of 1964, I read an item in *AD-1964*, the denominational magazine of the United Church of Christ, mentioning that the Board for Homeland Ministries was supporting a ministry to night people in San Francisco. The paragraph was brief and worded in such a way that made me believe that it was printed after the fact, that the minister had been called and the program was already under way. I wrote to Dr. Purd Dietz, the Executive Director of the Board, about some business pertaining to my Lincoln congregation, but added a paragraph indicating that I was pleased that they were supporting so innovative a ministry. I mentioned that I had spent a couple of years in San Francisco as a young sailor during World War II and felt that if there ever was a city in the country that needed such a ministry, it was San Francisco. Dr. Dietz replied to the question I had about my work in Lincoln and added, "I am glad that you have shown an interest in the San Francisco Night Ministry. I submitted your name as a candidate."

The Night Ministry Committee of the San Francisco Council of Churches soon wrote to me. After an exchange of letters and phone calls over the next several months, a conference call was held. They informed me that I had been chosen as one of two finalists. They invited me to San Francisco for a three-day meeting and interview with the entire committee. When I arrived back in Lincoln, a telegram was waiting for me saying that I had been chosen for the job. I was overjoyed and filled with enthusiasm!

When I was stationed on Treasure Island in the mid-1940s, San Francisco captured my heart—a wonderful city filled with vitality and energy. Born and raised hundreds of miles from either ocean, I appreciated the clean, salty breeze blowing in from the Pacific. I found the fog refreshing and I loved the long call of the foghorns that filled the night with mystery. Big ships came from all parts of the world, groping their way beneath the bridges. They fascinated me and filled my mind with romantic imaginings. Surely no city can be more seductive than this city, which legendary columnist Herb Caen dubbed "Baghdad-by-the-Bay." Like a dignified matriarch, San Francisco is a city of beauty in her pastel shades and sensuous swells. But serve her a few cocktails and turn the lights down low and she becomes as much of a seductress as any of her famous Gold Rush-era madams who hosted prostitution and gambling on her infamous Barbary Coast!

Since I was born and raised in Chicago, I was somewhat more street-wise than a lot of my clergy contemporaries but I was still naive about this new world opening before me. I thought back to 1940 when I decided to enter the ministry. I had created my own fantasy of how I thought clergy lived and acted, and became a prude in the most exaggerated sense of the word. Two things brought me out of this dream world and back to reality: the Navy (I enlisted in 1944) and a book, *Light the Dark Street,* by C. Kilmer Myers. Myers' book told of his work with gangs and street people while he was Vicar of St. Augustine's Chapel in New York City's Lower East Side. The book became my "bible" and Myers my mentor, leading me toward a ministry I never dreamed I would be

People came off the bus and sometimes into a new world.

called to fulfill. Myers later became the Episcopal Bishop of California, and I was able to cultivate our friendship in person.

Now the San Francisco Council of Churches was calling me to develop a ministry to night people. Euphoric when I first heard of the posting, I was now both challenged and frightened. It was new territory. Nothing exactly like it had been tried before. No textbooks or guides had been written to give me direction on how to begin work with so nebulous a population as those categorized as "night people." Novels had been written about people who functioned at night, including John Rechy's *City of Night*, but no psychological profiles existed to describe the people who made up the night population. Fr. Bob Owens, an Episcopal priest, was just beginning to work with the entertainment community in Old Town of Chicago and Pierre De Latre had just left North Beach in San Francisco where he worked on upper Grant Street with the Beatniks (the poets and writers who lived in North Beach and used the City Lights Book Store as their unofficial meeting place). But these were specialists. There was no general ministry to the entire night population.

I had to find out for myself who these "night people" were. I quickly discovered that most of my assumptions were wrong. More importantly, I found that the vast majority of night people had the same emotions, the same frustrations and fears, the same sense of loneliness and isolation experienced

Arriving at the bus terminal could be exciting, but more often it turned out to be a destructive experience.

by their sisters and brothers who functioned during the day.

The night I began was a typical Saturday evening in San Francisco. The air was damp and chilly, unlike the Augusts I spent in Kansas and Nebraska. I had no problem spotting the tourists. They were the ones shivering in shorts and T-shirts, or running back to their hotels to escape what they considered unseasonably cold weather. It was clear to me, though, that the majority of this throng was inside somewhere.

Standing on this street corner, I couldn't help but wonder what I was going to do with these people whose activities were couched in darkness. Did most of them live on the dark side of the law, hiding in the shadows, conducting their nefarious activities in dark alleys and flea-bitten hotels? Certainly there were those whose activities were questionable. Some of the people who passed me were prostitutes and pimps. How many walking the streets at this time of night were really drug addicts and pushers? Could I tell by looking who were pickpockets and skid-row alcoholics?

In the midst of this marching throng was the other side of the night population—those who were often neglected by "respectable society." Some, whom I eventually came to know and count as friends, were bus drivers and bartenders, telephone operators and ticket-takers, the cops on the beat, the performers on the stage, the waiters and waitresses who dished up food and poured coffee by the gallon all night long, the nurses in the operating rooms and cab drivers on the street. They worked all night and slept all day—out of sync with society and out of harmony with their own body rhythms! They often felt isolated from those who worked "normal" hours, from the Church, and even from their own families.

Before I found my place on the street at night, I contacted as many daytime service agencies as I could. I discovered that there were about three hundred and fifty agencies (including churches) that offered a smorgasbord of services to meet almost any need, but most of them closed their offices at five or six p.m. The Salvation Army was available until ten o'clock. The Travelers Aid booths at the airport and bus station were also open until ten p.m. and sometimes until midnight, if they could find volunteers to work those hours. A few hospitals had emergency rooms but they handled only health or injury cases. Only two of them, San Francisco General and Mt. Sinai, provided psychiatric help, and then only for those with acute or life-threatening problems.

The primary goal of the Night Ministry was not to bring about social change. The Ministry was able to contribute information about night people and their activities because of the statistics it accumulated and the in-the-field experience garnered. This assisted other agencies to include the needs of the night people in their work.

San Francisco had grown like no other American city. The Gold Rush brought thousands of people to California and especially to San Francisco. Many were headed to the gold fields to seek their fortune in that elusive Mother Lode that few ever saw. Others stayed in the City to make it one of the most wild and woolly in the country—a reputation it has maintained for one hundred and fifty years.

Émigrés came not only from the United States, but from all parts of the world. These new immigrants formed their own "urban villages" within the borders of the larger city. San Francisco became fragmented into a number of small social and ethnic enclaves. The most radical ghetto was Chinatown, confined by zoning ordinances to a prescribed area. Eventually, these borders began to break down—mainly because of the "Americanization" of other immigrants, and especially of their children. They no longer wanted to be Italians in America, but Italian-Americans. They became better educated than their parents. In their schools they mingled with children from other neighborhoods. Sometimes to the consternation of their parents, they often married outside their ethnic or religious background. As their incomes improved, they moved out of the "old neighborhood" to suburbs where the diversity is even more pronounced. They went to the same schools and churches and socialized with the children of immigrants from almost every part of the world and it no longer made a difference. This migration left holes in the old neighborhoods. North Beach was once the home of the Italian community. As they moved out, the ones waiting to fill the empty flats and apartments were their adjacent neighbors, the Chinese. Once the breach was made, the changed laws could no longer confine them to a designated geographic area and the Chinese moved quickly into other neighborhoods of the City as well.

Young married adults were attracted to San Francisco because job opportunities were plentiful. With housing costs among the highest in the nation, large mortgage payments made it necessary for both partners to work. Time for non-work related activities was limited. Many of these couples did not choose to spend their discretionary time in church activities. Couples postponed having children. As a result, there was a diminished interest in educational issues. Young parents had little time to participate in their children's activities such as PTA, scouts, or religious schools. Their spiritual journey was often sidetracked, resulting in the lack of ethical support that the Church and educational institutions could bring to their lives.

The surge of traditional European immigrants was past. People from other continents and other colors supplanted them. East Indians and Pakistanis had almost taken over the small hotel industry in San Francisco. At one time the area where that industry was centered was Irish Catholic. More recently, the Mission District became a place where Spanish-speaking refugees from Mexico, Central America, and South America came seeking political refuge and financial improvement among the existing large Spanish-speaking population. When one community moved out, another moved in to fill the void.

San Francisco has always been an open city, which not only tolerated different lifestyles, but embraced them. The City accepted the diverse and even international people brought to its harbor by the Gold Rush. The World Wars changed the City's demographics and introduced Blacks because of its need for a labor force. Servicemen who had fallen in love with the City returned in large numbers to establish their families in San Francisco. The Chinese were well integrated into the City. The late 1950s began the influx of young gays, and runaways, predecessors of the "flower children" of the 1960s. The actress Sarah Bernhardt, when questioned about the outlandish behavior of some San Franciscans, is reputed to have replied, "I don't care what they do, as long as they don't do it in the streets and scare the horses." This became the City's credo.

In such a place, in August of 1964, I began a ministry to "night people." In 1967 a study/evaluation was conducted by the Bureau of Community Research in Berkeley. Authors Thomas R. McFaul and Alan P. Farr succinctly described the new ministry in their report titled, *The San Francisco Night Ministry*:

> If one were to catch a glimpse of the Night Minister, as he is called from one end of San Francisco to the other, as he confronts new situations and persons, each with his own unique problems or concerns, one would almost certainly conclude that here is a completely spontaneous and flexible ministry. Here is a ministry which is "going where the action is," with no institutional restraints. Such indeed is the case.

The Night Ministry was intentionally designed that way. It was designed to confront the problems of nightlife in San Francisco as they occurred, when they occurred, and where they occurred.

CHAPTER 2

When Darkness Comes

My first night on the street was one of total tension. I wore a clerical collar and walked the Tenderloin streets alone. Will the collar be a help or a hindrance? Will I come through the night in this most disreputable section of the City without being mugged, robbed, beaten up, or killed? I was paralyzed with anticipation, excitement and fear. How could I make contact? How would those who need help contact me?

Timing would be critical. Once contact was made would I be able to persuade the person needing help that I was not there to judge or condemn, but to support and help however I was able? Was it possible to work with people with so many needs without being an enabler? Eventually, when I had a primitive "beeper," and a telephone call-in line manned by volunteers to help me reach those in need, I got used to the fact that I could seldom prepare myself for the next call because I never knew what that next call would be. Later in the Ministry, when seminarians came to work with me, I counseled them to approach every call with an open and non-judgmental mind, to listen, not only to hear what the caller had to say, but also to build on that, to love, loving even those who were not too loveable.

On that first official night on the streets, I did have one contact. Just before leaving home, I received a message from Suicide Prevention. The night clerk at a small but posh hotel on Bush Street called regarding a woman who was acting "strangely" and talking of suicide. This, my first call, was to be the most difficult of all, and the kind which continued to cause me apprehension through all the years I spent on the street.

I had never counseled a suicidal person before. Whatever expertise I had in this area was academic. I was as frightened for myself as for the young woman I was called upon to "save." I didn't know the woman. I had no background material on her, not even her name or how she looked. If someone called for counseling when I was in a traditional parish, I had a file of information on that person and could prepare myself for a counseling session, could consider the problem beforehand, and could plan an approach, even, perhaps, a solution.

How would I approach her? What would I say? Would I inadvertently say something that would throw her over the edge or, by the grace of God, could I say those words that would save her life for this one night at least? I was to relive that first experience with every subsequent suicide call and each time I subjected myself to the same litany of questions.

Josh, the hotel's night clerk, was a college student who was almost petrified by the drama going on upstairs and by the fear that it was somehow his fault. He was certain he would be fired because this happened on his watch. "We operate a respectable hotel. Nothing like this is supposed to happen here," he nervously told me several times. He shared the little background material he had: the woman's name was Shirley; she arrived from the East that evening by plane and came to the hotel by airport shuttle. She was attractive and well dressed, had expensive-looking matched luggage. There was nothing unusual about her actions until she got to her room and called the desk almost hysterically threatening to kill herself.

I went to Shirley's room but received no answer to my knock. I went back down to the desk and persuaded Josh to give me the master key (he was sure this was something else that most certainly would get him fired). Shirley's was not a "run-of-the-mill" room. It was beautifully furnished and expensively decorated, lighted by a single bed lamp with an aged parchment shade that gave a soft warm glow to the room. Shirley was lying on the bed on her back, looking very much as though she had fallen into a restful sleep. She was

It isn't always easy to start your day in the middle of the night, when darkness comes.

unresponsive to my voice or touch. Her breathing was shallow and her skin showed some discoloration. I immediately called for an ambulance, and had her rushed to the hospital. The ER team pumped her stomach and held her seventy two hours for the psychiatric evaluation required by California law. As soon as she was released and returned to the hotel she called me. Her call initiated a counseling relationship, which lasted throughout my entire ministry on the streets. She never attempted suicide again, although she did sometimes contemplate it. The desk clerk was not fired and we remained friends for the next two years until he finished his undergraduate work, appropriately enough, in abnormal psychology.

I began my actual and symbolic descent down the hill into the Tenderloin or, as it felt at the moment, the Jaws of Hell!!

A young woman walked by and smiled seductively. She was attractive in spite of her heavy make-up, wearing high heels and a bouffant wig. She stood about six-feet-two. She was stylishly dressed, but something didn't quite add up. Her shoulders were much too broad and her hips too narrow. Or perhaps she stood out because she was a little unsteady in her spike heels. Noticing me watching, she turned, swinging her hips seductively, and asked in a very deep voice, "Want a date, honey?" Like Dorothy in the Wizard of Oz, I suddenly realized that I wasn't in Kansas anymore. This was to be the first of the on-going contacts I had with innumerable transsexuals and transvestites over the next twelve years.

She introduced herself as Bonny Brae, the "Queen of the Tenderloin." She asked what a priest was doing on a corner like this at this time of night. I tried, as succinctly as possible, to explain who I was and what I intended to do in this neighborhood. When I finished, she said, "You ain't gonna see nothing, honey, unless I show it to you." In just a few words she laid down the ground rules for an enjoyable relationship, lasting for years.

She grabbed my arm and we set off toward Eddy and Mason streets, up a flight of stairs into a dark and dingy club with a small and cluttered stage at one end. Everyone seemed to know Bonny, or wanted to; I navigated with some difficulty through her admirers. The club didn't have a liquor license, but offered watered down coffee, two-dollar soft drinks and day old sandwiches. The performers were tired old "queens" who were not funny and no longer attractive. A few told me they were "retired" from Finnochios, a popular gay nightclub located on Broadway.

Young Black men in outlandish attire milled about, flaunting their new-found sexuality. It was one of the few places where I met gay Blacks. They did not even hang out on Mason and Market at the "meat rack," a pedestrian barrier on the corner of Market and Mason used by hustlers. It was their way of saying, "FUCK YOU!" to disapproving parents, the Church, and the rest of society. I seldom saw Black hustlers except in Chuckers, a rough bar catering as much to drugs as to sex. The thought hit me that if this is what the gay world was all about, I may never make any inroads.

When Bonny decided that she had shown me off enough, we headed for the streets again. I hadn't the slightest clue as to where we were headed next. Bonny almost fell down the stairs, teetering on her high heels. She led me toward the Gilded Cage, holding court along the way, eating up the adulation of her admirers who told her how beautiful she was.

The Cage was an attractive bar filled with middle-aged men dressed in suits and ties. They could use the spot to pick up hustlers but were certainly not ones themselves. The bar was long and located to the left of the front door. At the far end was a small, almost puppet-sized stage. Bonny introduced me to the main attraction, Charles Pierce, and his partner Dante. Charles billed himself as a "Male Actress." He was a good comedienne and an excellent impressionist. Later, as he got to know me better, he worked me into his good-natured jibes against society, and the Church.

Bonny pulled me into the street again. She was getting tired (and a little drunk) and began to stumble. We went on to the Caboose, a diner catering to a rough and hostile crowd. A couple of boys, trying to ingratiate themselves with Bonny, offered us their booth. I ordered what must have been my fiftieth cup of coffee. No matter how urgent my need for a restroom, I hesitated to go. I found it difficult to stand at a urinal next to someone in full drag. Eventually, I overcame that "hang-up."

We had just settled in, when a well-dressed young man in his mid-twenties squeezed in next to me. He shook my hand and introduced himself as Robert. A part of my education was to learn that men in the gay world would seldom, if ever, use their last name until they got to know the other person better. He seemed intelligent and well read, definitely not a hustler or street person. I introduced him to Bonny but was quickly corrected. "My name is *Bonny BRAE*," she said. That was the last time I called her just "Bonny."

Robert told us he was from the Northwest side of Chicago, which gave us something in common. He was a senior anthropology major at U.C. Berkeley. Just when I thought I was gaining entrée to a more "normal" gay segment of the City, Robert jumped from his seat and almost screamed, "Oh my God! Oh my God! You're a priest! I thought you were wearing a turtle-neck sweater."

Thankfully, we rested a bit. It was now a little after 2:00 a.m. I was exhausted, but Bonny announced, "I'm not finished with you yet." We took off for O'Farrell Street, up an alley behind the Gilded Cage, and down a short flight of stairs into Pearls, an after-hours club catering to gay minors. Bonny pulled me past the doorman and into the club. It was simply decorated, but a welcoming haven for those who frequented the place. The "witching hour" when the bars closed at 2:00 a.m. was past and Bonny had not yet "scored," making a successful sexual contact. She needed to hit the streets before she missed the last desperate souls leaving the bars. Before she said "Good night," she introduced me to Lou, the manager, who instructed his doorman not to bill me for the cover charge when I visited. The next morning Lou called the Council of Churches' office to check my credentials. When the secretary told him I was legitimate he thanked her and said, "You know we can't be too careful; we get all kinds of kooks in here!" It was good to know that he really cared about the teenaged kids who came to his club.

The rest of the night was comparatively calm. I received some sidelong glances and snide or angry remarks in a few bars and gay clubs. One bartender asked me to leave. He said I was bad for business. But the manager stepped in and said that I was welcome there any time. After a few months, when the bartender found that I wasn't there to convert, we became friends. That Christmas he gave me a pair of cuff links inlaid with the Christian symbol of the fish. He was Jewish.

Some prostitutes propositioned me; but another "sister" would say, "Don't work him, girl. He's a Father!"

Fifteen- to eighteen-year-old male hustlers were crowded together sitting on the "meat rack." Some were confused when I approached them. They thought I was just another "john," a customer looking to score, priest or not. Some were intimidated and angry, some welcoming; the majority simply ignored me. Most of the hustlers felt that I would interfere with their business because a "trick" (another term for customer) would hesitate to stop his car and negotiate if I were standing nearby.

As I became a regular figure on the street, these boys came to know me and to share at least a part of their lives with me. After a time I eventually became a father figure for many of them who knew nothing about a caring father or a supporting home life. On occasion a very young and innocent kid who was not yet "street wise" would ask if I would take him home with me and become his father. Few had a satisfactory male role model and I had difficulty in persuading them that I cared about their welfare without expecting sexual favors in exchange.

Secundo, a handsome nineteen-year old Mexican boy, insisted that I come to his room so he could show me how much he thought of me. I felt a sadness that the only way this personable young man thought he could relate to me was sexually. Even after I rejected his offer, we remained friends until he disappeared from the streets.

Pearls became one of my regular stops. After these boys realized I wasn't there to preach or to solicit sex, they opened up and were eager to talk. Most of the clientele were male, but a handful of girls also hung out at Pearls. It was not unusual for both boys and girls ("fruit flies") to line up at my table to share their anxiety about their life-style, or other problems confronting them. These girls were called "fruit flies" because they preferred to spend time with gay boys, feeling safer with them because they didn't have to fend off sexual advances when on a date. The gay boys liked the girls because they could attend straight functions without being accused of being gay.

One of the young men was Tom, the 19-year-old son of a friend who was a prominent minister in the City. Even though his father was accepting of his sexuality, Tom was not. He felt that he could never live up to his father's image. While traveling with friends he took his own life. There has always been a high rate of suicide among gay teenagers.

One of my "regulars" was David, an intelligent, handsome, young Jewish boy whose parents could not accept his lifestyle. They asked him to either change or leave their home. His grandmother took him in. She told him, "I don't care whether you're homosexual or not. But if you insist that you are,

I'm going to make you the best damned homosexual in the City." He liked being with me but seldom talked to me when I was at Pearls. "I don't want these queens to think that I'm having any problems." We met in the balcony of a cafeteria on Powell Street. David was a straightforward kid who never hesitated to share the most intimate aspects of his life with me. He eventually disappeared from the scene and I never heard what happened to him.

The City, much like a harlot, is a thing of beauty on the surface, but often a cacophony of discontent underneath. I drove down Market Street looking for a phone. The neon signs, blended in beauty when seen from Twin Peaks, the high hills in the middle of the City that afford panoramic views, now seemed obscene as they flashed "Bar" or "Arcade" or "Topless" in my face. I knew that behind the many twinkling windows at that hour, there was not always laughter and gaiety. Often there was illness, drunkenness, strife and the ever-present loneliness.

CHAPTER 3

Everybody's Favorite City

San Francisco is a city of beauty and a sight to behold! Her tiny alleys, excellent restaurants, and lovely pastel-hued homes make her "Everybody's Favorite City." Her bawdy history, cosmopolitan air, and cultural advantages appeal to visitor and resident alike. But in spite of the fact that San Francisco is one of the best loved cities in the world, one does not have to scratch the surface too deeply to discern the same problems found in other metropolitan areas, or to discover negative characteristics which are peculiar to her alone.

Few American cities receive as much poetic attention as does San Francisco. Innumerable books and articles have been written extolling her beauty and commending her charm. This City, at first glance, fascinates. From a distance her undulating hills look absolutely sensuous. But every aspect of life has its shadow side. In the darkness of the night she becomes a seductive siren, luring and teasing the passions. A closer look reveals a tired old madam desperately hanging on to a fading past. Even that wonderful, tourist-attracting Chinatown with its mysterious, shadowy alleys, its fun-filled shops and unsurpassable restaurants, is deceptive. How fortunate to have so exciting a community in the midst of the City. But wait—take a closer look. To go past the bright and colorful façade, through one of those dark alleys and up a stairway, is to enter into an unbelievable world of misery and poverty!

My second night, without Bonnie Brae to introduce me around, was more difficult. I had to wait for people to approach me. I began, as I had on the previous evening, in the Tenderloin. The first part of the night was quiet except for a few contacts with young hustlers hanging out at Turk and Mason streets. They abandoned me quickly when I made it clear that I didn't intend to "score."

I decided to have my "lunch" in Chinatown. I took off, looking for a Chinese restaurant recommended by Matthew Fong, a minister friend of mine. I eventually found the place in a deserted alley, down a flight of stairs. My wild imagination and preconceived stereotypes told me that this once was an opium den or a meeting room for a tong (a secret society or fraternal organization, formerly notorious for gang warfare).

The restaurant was nicely appointed and crowded with Chinese customers. This was a good sign. I sat at the counter, rather than at a table, to be more accessible. My waitress was young and attractive. She asked me a lot of questions about what I, a priest, was doing in this neighborhood at that hour (after 2:00 a.m.). This was a common question. I explained as briefly as I could, what and who I was. Mistaking me for a Roman Catholic priest, she asked if I would talk to anyone or did they have to be Catholic. When I said, "Yes, I will talk to anyone," she went through the kitchen and out the back door. A short time later she returned with a request that I talk to her grandfather. She gave me directions to their room. It sounded simple until I started looking for it through a maze of convoluted alleys and dark, deserted streets.

With the help of a restaurant worker who was emptying trash, I found the doorway. I opened the door, and entered a dark hallway. I walked up a steep flight of narrow stairs toward a dim, bare light bulb hanging from the ceiling. Standing under this bulb was a dignified Chinese gentleman in a dazzlingly white T-shirt and black pants. He was regal, even in this simple garb. I envisioned him wearing a long, embroidered silk gown. He ushered me into an unbelievable room, not cluttered or dirty, but packed with boxes neatly stacked in every possible crevice, and on one wall reaching the ceiling. A bunk bed and a single bed neatly filled the remaining space. Six adults lived in this tiny cubicle. They cooked in a communal kitchen down the hall. He

Everybody's Favorite City.

signaled for me to sit on the bunk bed while he and his younger granddaughter sat on the single bed. Embarrassed at having to turn to a stranger for help, this proud gentleman further humbled himself by having his English-speaking grandchild translate for him.

Ordinarily he would have handled this family matter himself. Both his son and daughter-in-law spent most of their time working. His granddaughter had an after-school job at the restaurant and was doing well. The problem was Charlie, his sixteen-year old grandson. Charlie was failing in school and spent little time with his family. He had joined one of the newly formed gangs that were fighting against the influx of Chinese young people emigrating from Hong Kong. The newcomers were perceived as taking jobs from the American-born Chinese youth.

I asked to meet with the young man and we set a time for several nights later. The grandfather assured me Charlie would be there. Charlie came but was uncooperative. He saw no reason to meet with a counselor, especially a white one. "Nothin's wrong with me!" I gave him several Chinese referrals although I was certain he would make no effort to follow through. But he surprised me.

Through the love of his grandfather and the help of understanding counselors he was able to break from the gang. This incident taught me a valuable lesson. Young people sometimes want a way out but don't know what steps to take. The last time I saw the grandfather, he bowed low, thanked me and offered to pay me. I refused; he bowed again and departed. The picture left in my mind was that of a courageous and proud old man willing to risk his dignity and anything else to save his grandson who was lost between two diametrically opposed cultures.

From Chinatown it was only a few blocks up Grant Avenue to fun-filled Broadway with its bright lights and wild topless shows. How could there be tragedy here where there was so much laughter? But how much of that laughter was real and how much of it was just a cover-up for the hurt within?

One of my regular stops became Enrico's, a coffee house on Broadway. It had an open front, making it possible to sit at a table and see all the action taking place on the street. Enrico's was a hangout for celebrities and street people alike. I tried to show up after the bars closed when people looked for one more stop before heading home. Broadway club performers also frequented Enrico's looking for a place to relax before going to their apartments.

I was sitting at Enrico's contemplating the events of the night and savoring a cup of rich, hot chocolate, when an attractive young woman asked if she could join me. There were other empty tables nearby, so I assumed she was coming with her own agenda.

Jan was a divorcée with two children, one in preschool, and the other in first grade. Her ex-husband was a deadbeat dad who made no effort to support the children or even visit them. She was a junior at San Francisco State University where she was majoring in sociology, with the hope of becoming a counselor of women in situations similar to her own. In order to support her family and pay her way through school with work that fit her schedule, she had taken a job in one of the Broadway clubs as a topless waitress. The pay was adequate and the hours made it possible to spend time with the children. As she came to trust and respect me, she asked that I never come into her club. She said, "I would be too embarrassed for you to see me topless!"

Later in the year, I told her about a family I picked up the day before Thanksgiving. I had housed them and supplied them with the makings for a traditional dinner. Jan, this woman, whom most "respectable" people would have shunned, said, "Don, don't do that again. If ever you come across a stranded family, call me anytime, day or night. I have an extra room and even an extra crib. The place is yours when you need it." I never received a more generous and open-handed offer as I did from this single mother doing the best she could to keep her little family together.

"Everybody's Favorite City?" Then why is the suicide rate one of the highest in the country? Why are alcohol and drug related diseases, like cirrhosis of the liver, hepatitis, and other problems, higher than the national average?

San Francisco is a night city. Tourists wanting to gain the most from their visit, make the rounds of the attractions. They roam the streets until the early morning hours. But, at some point they return, first to the anonymity of a hotel room with a pick-up, and then home.

Stranded transients can become overwhelmed by frustration and fear when helping agency offices are closed. They need the same support at night that is available to those who can access it during the day. Many residents suffer too—the aged living in cheap rooming houses, single young adults seeking company to curb their loneliness, and night workers. These people are out making the streets almost as active during the night as they are at high noon. The same quaint alleys and interesting courts that charm the tourist in the daylight, terrorize the lonely in darkness. North Beach and Chinatown draw the pleasure-seeker but when the lights dim, the bands stop playing, and the last discotheque closes, the excitement of the night fades away, and loneliness and hopelessness set in. The entertainer, the topless waitress, the last of the merry-makers find the oppression of their dingy rooms and the futility of meaningless lives more than they can face alone. Daytime can be tolerated and the feeling of loneliness and isolation can be submerged in the workaday world. But night always comes, and so do weekends. Both bring the fear of being alone which manifests itself in the myriad problems that were brought to the Night Minister every night.

I could not have functioned effectively without the sixty or more volunteers who worked in teams of two each night handling the phone calls that came to the Night Ministry office. I was never in that office, other than to open it at 9:30 p.m. to let the volunteers in for the night and to close it at 6:00 a.m. to allow them to go home.

After getting the volunteers settled, I hit the streets, on the lookout for whatever situation needed my attention. Mine was a ministry of presence. Rarely did I intrude or involve myself with a person unless some signal was given or my interference was necessary for the person's safety.

The volunteers handled those calls that didn't need my personal attention: the lonely person needing someone to talk to or those needing a referral to an agency that could help them in the morning. Those were the days of live operators on the phone and live agents available at the bus depot or airport. A countless number of people would make calls to these agents just to hear the sound of another human voice. Some of these callers were referred to the Night Ministry for follow-up.

When an emergency call came in from someone who needed me in person, I could be reached via a primitive beeper. I contacted the office to get the number of the person calling and then called him or her directly. It was slow and sometimes tedious but it got the job done. When I was not on a call, I simply wandered the streets looking for trouble. I would stop at the bus depot, all-night restaurants, bars, and nightclubs—anyplace frequented by people looking for escape. Sometimes someone would hear or read about my work and he or she would also wander the streets hoping to find me.

The focus of my ministry became the Tenderloin, that intimate forty-five square block area just south of Union Square inhabited by an estimated 50,000 people. I chose this section of the City in which to work because it was the one area open all night. Some action could always be caught there. Herb Caen called it a "place of broken dreams, of frozen screams, of strangers rubbing elbows." It is a different place today with a whole new set of problems than when I knew it. It is an area a million miles away from the San Francisco Tony Bennett sings about where, "little cable cars climb halfway to the stars." It was, and probably still is, the most cosmopolitan area in the entire city, calling people from all parts of the world and catering to every taste in food and flesh the mind can imagine.

This cosmopolitan atmosphere was exemplified by Sam's, the German HofBrau, David's for Kosher food, Paoli's for Italian cuisine, and Minerva's for wonderful Greek delicacies, loud boisterous music, and dancing. There was the Grubstake with its "boy-girls" (young male teens dressed in somewhat feminine clothing) contemptuously eyeing those who seemed unfriendly or unsympathetic.

Open-air, all-night restaurants lined Market Street, where one could pick up a quick bite or buy a quick pick-up. Eddy Street was teeming with leather-coated, mini-skirted girls, smiling suggestively or seductively asking if you'd like to have some fun. On Taylor Street, the uninitiated might mistake the streetwalkers for women, and sailors soon learned that they needed a scorecard to tell who the real girls were.

As the sun snuggled down behind Twin Peaks, and the shadows lengthened and the canyons of the city streets grew dark, a whole new population emerged. The fun-seekers descended and the Tenderloin took on a new personality. Dirt and dinginess were hidden in dark and sympathetic shadows. Glaring marquees screamed for attention. Bright-eyed lights flashed alluringly: "SEX-SEX-SEX." Both the hookers and the hustlers vied for a favorite spot on the street, and the body into which God breathed the breath of Life was debased and exploited in honor of a few dirty dollars.

When the rushing and bustling of the daylight hours faded, the hookers and the hustlers smiled; even the pimps became friendly and talkative. Barkers slapped potential customers on the back and told of unheard pleasures hidden just behind the curtained doors of "Everybody's Favorite City." The fun capital of the world! But, as columnist Herb Caen described, should one find a crack in the façade or look behind the vapid faces of the frenzied fun-seekers, he or she would find torture and torment, pain and anguish gathered together in this miserable microcosm called the Tenderloin:

Like all great cities, San Francisco takes on a seductive glitter and glow after dark. Red tail lights swim up the hills, white headlights skitter down. The new buildings, so brutal by day, are bathed in a warm glow; even the signs seem less ugly as they spring to light. The night is a time of whispers and shadows, silhouettes behind drawn curtains, pale yellow reflections in Chinatown alleys. The bridges reach out fancifully to nowhere and everywhere. Smell of smoke, incense, perfume and rot, sound of laughter, guitars and misery. The night owl, the nocturnal drifter, is neurotically at home, his face sallow, eyes neon bright. As the great hands of the Ferry Building clock droop past midnight, he keeps reminding himself that anything can happen.

If you really want to see the city, leave Union Square, quickly pass through Chinatown, get away from Ghiardelli Square! Forget Fisherman's Wharf, and take a stroll on the seamy side. Desert the sanctuaries of security, and you will quickly discover that all of life is not a cabaret; as soon as the last song is sung and the last dance is danced, the painted smile fades away, and souls, seemingly hardened and untouchable, almost scream for relationship and meaning. To the outsider, the Tenderloin may appear to be a hopeless Sodom and Gomorrah. "Destroy it. Tear it down! Turn it over to urban renewal!" they cry. But for those who love people, what a gold mine of opportunity is there.

CHAPTER 4

Faceless, Voiceless, Powerless—and Gay

San Francisco has a large homosexual population and for years had been considered the "gay capital" of America. In 1964, homosexuality was still in the closet as far as agency help was concerned. It was considered a mental illness. As Thomas McFaul and Allen Farr state in their 1967 report, *The San Francisco Night Ministry*:

> Like any other minority group, the homophile community is by no means monolithic. There are sub-cultures within this community. Many of the homosexuals are "hustlers." These persons are predominately teenagers. Some are as young as twelve or thirteen years of age; others may be in their mid-twenties. The median age, according to one source, is around seventeen. These persons, in order to support themselves financially, are compelled to sell their bodies.
>
> The major group of homosexuals is adults over twenty-one years of age. These persons are independent, hold jobs and are usually financially self-supporting. Because of the stigma which this society places on homosexual behavior, these individuals, especially if they have jobs, have to protect their personal identity and hide their feelings for fear of intimidation, harassment, exposure, or even blackmail.

Before 1965 there were few organizations to protect homosexuals from social intimidation and harassment. There were the Matachine Society and

"One" (both national organizations), and The Tavern Guild, a loosely knit local organization of gay bar owners and managers. None of them provided emergency counseling services nor did they have the political power to speak out against the oppression of gays and lesbians. Even as late as 1964, the term "gay" was not widely used by the general public. According to the McFaul and Farr study:

> The Society For Individual Rights and the Daughters of Bilitis [were two] organizations [that] were created for the purpose of giving the gay individual a sense of dignity and worth, to help him or her become integrated into the community and to attempt to educate the public about homosexuality and change unquestioned, highly prejudiced and stereotyped attitudes about homosexual behavior. The Council on Religion and the Homosexual, and a number of other organizations, [were] also developed to perform a similar function. Within the gay community, there [was] hostility between some of the older homosexuals and the younger hustlers. Some of the older persons [felt] that the reputation of the hustler negated the positive image they [were] trying to create through their public relations efforts.

To the general public before World War II, gay bars were "queer bars" or "homosexual" bars if you wanted to be polite. I first became acquainted with the term "gay" when I was in high school and worked closely with George in the Art Department. He was still closeted but open to those he could trust. At that time, during the 1930s, you had to be gay to understand whom the word identified or have a gay friend who trusted you enough to share at least some of their underground life. George eventually became a principal dancer with the Ballet Russe de Monte Carlo. We remained in touch into the 1990s.

Part of my job description was to begin a dialogue with the gay community. This segment of society had been totally neglected—faceless in our congregations, voiceless in our communities, and powerless in our politics. The Night Ministry was determined to work with and accept gays and lesbians on its governing board and to present their cause before the congregations, which looked to us for program leadership.

Even though San Francisco always had a large gay population, it was only within recent years that gay neighborhoods began to emerge. The Castro District and Polk Gulch are relatively recent developments dating back about forty years, to the early 1960s. Though other cities still found gays a problem, the "City" had been working through the tensions between straight and gay lifestyles for years. The City was dealing more creatively with them than was any other American city. It was the first major city to elect an openly gay person to the Board of Supervisors, Harvey Milk, in 1977.

Then, in 1978, eleven months into his term, Harvey Milk was assassinated while in office. He was a gay activist and owner of a camera shop on Castro Street. Harvey was popular in the gay community, which encouraged him to run for a spot on the Board of Supervisors. He was elected along with Dan White. Dan was the only anti-gay member of the Board. He struggled with his feelings of being the only conservative on a liberal Board. He handed in his resignation, but then reconsidered and asked his letter to be withdrawn. Mayor George Moscone, a straight, liberal mayor, refused to reverse the resignation. Hearing this news at home, White got out his service revolver (he was formerly a police officer), went to City Hall and climbed through a window to avoid security at the front entrance. He went to the mayor's office and killed him. He then reloaded his gun, went to the office of Harvey Milk, and killed him also.

Dan White was found guilty, but because of "Diminished Capacity" from eating too many "Twinkies" the day of the killings, he was convicted of manslaughter and sentenced to a seven-year prison term. After this "Twinkie verdict," thousands of gays stormed City Hall and a riot ensued. This was the Stonewall of the West Coast, reflecting the riots at the Stonewall Inn in New York City where gays fought back against police harassment, triggering the gay liberation movement in June 1969. Dan White served five years of his sentence and sometime after his release committed suicide by carbon monoxide poisoning in the garage of his family home in San Francisco.

In 1964, homosexuality was still considered a mental illness. Even in a city like San Francisco, prejudice existed against gays. Gay bashing was practiced by policemen who called it "curbside justice" and by teenage toughs who saw it as a Saturday night entertainment to prove their masculinity.

Don, a minister friend of mine, returned home after a board meeting. He took his dog out and while walking along Dolores Street, a car-load of young men looking for a gay to beat up (a sport for young punks), jumped from the car and struck him with a pipe. His skull was fractured in several places. He was hospitalized and in a coma for months. It was not known whether he would live or die. He survived but never quite recovered from the trauma of the senseless beating by the toughs who labeled him a gay man simply because he was walking his dog late at night along Dolores Street, which bordered on the Castro District and was known as a cruising place for gays.

Throughout my ministry, people referred to homosexuality as a "sexual preference." Whenever this happened, I invited him or her to spend time with me on the streets. This gave them an opportunity to meet, first hand, this segment of our population, who were ridiculed and brutalized by those who had no understanding of the rejection many of these men and women must endure. As a result of the attitude of the population, which included their family, suicide for many seemed the only way out, especially among gay teens. Not surprisingly, the homosexual suicide rate was higher than that of the general population. On more than one occasion, I counseled men who, under pressure from their families, married, believing marriage would "cure" them. I tried to persuade anyone who believed that homosexuality was a choice, that no one would consciously choose it. It was a lifestyle that often brought with it pain and rejection.

Toward the end of 1964, representatives of the Tavern Guild (the loosely

Being faceless, voteless, powerless and gay in the 1950s could be a lonely road.

knit local organization of gay bar owners and managers) and the Daughters of Bilitis (the social action group, whose emphasis was working with lesbians) joined with Chuck Lewis (representing the Night Ministry and Lutherans Concerned) and Ted McIlvenna (from the Glide Foundation) to meet with the police chief and a representative from the community relations office of the Police Department. The purpose was to secure permission to hold a drag ball on January 1, 1965, as a fundraiser for the Council on Religion and the Homosexual. Permission was granted and a promise was made not to harass the partygoers.

At eight o'clock the night of the ball, I received an urgent call from Chuck, asking me to come to California Hall, where the dance was being held. I arrived to find complete chaos. A string of police vans lined the street with klieg lights aimed at the entrance to the hall. The police were photographing the participants, ridiculing and harassing anyone even vaguely sympathetic to those going in or coming out of the Ball. "How would you like your daughter to marry one of them?" a policeman asked. "How does your wife feel about your defending these queers?" snarled another.

This was a time when a gay person could be fired if his or her sexual orientation became known. The prospect of their pictures showing up in the morning paper was terrifying for many of the participants. On the night of the ball, volunteers who were working with the gay community escorted partygoers out of the hall. They attempted to maintain the anonymity of the participants by throwing coats over their heads, while they escorted them through the police lines. The police threatened to arrest the volunteers, which we suggested they do. But they weren't interested in further dulling their own already tarnished image.

The next morning, a press conference was held at Glide Memorial Church with a number of clergy representatives. Out of this meeting came a stronger voice in support of gay rights. Chuck Lewis was one of these voices. The Council on Religion and the Homosexual became an effective influence in working for gay rights and the Christian support of gays and lesbians.

Before I began work as Night Minister, the City's large gay population served as an incentive for gay migration. Just as hippies had been lured to this open-minded city, which welcomed them, so gays came to San Francisco, expecting to find a haven. Stories abound of young teenage gays on the loose because their parents were glad to get rid of them. They came from all over the country, from big cities and small towns, some into drugs before they came, or with the excited anticipation of being turned on after they arrived.

They were scared, they were isolated, and they were lonely. They pretended to be sophisticated. They acted cool, but still welcomed the chance to talk to someone they could trust. The Night Ministry became the clearing in the jungle where they could regain their perspective and take a new compass reading for redirecting their lives. Eager to trust, they were often burned in the process. In their meandering across the country they met at national parks and at desert campgrounds, at crossroads and at communes. They shared pot and a lot of stories. Someone would say, "Hey, I've got a cool friend in San Francisco. Get in touch when you get there and you can crash with him." But somehow the address never materialized and the crash pad was non-existent. Young gays were frequently exploited along the way. Once they reached the City, exploitation increased. Some found their only means of support was to sell their bodies.

Jim was seventeen. He was hitchhiking to San Francisco with two girls from his high school class. Because he was gay he came because of the "Gay Scene." The two girls hoped to link up with the hippies. Somewhere on an isolated road in Nevada, a truck driver and his partner raped both of the girls. When Jim made an effort to protect them, they raped him, too, and beat him. The three were left stranded in the desert without their backpacks or any money. When they got to the City, they went to the YMCA for help. The night clerk called me. I was able to arrange housing for a few days until they contacted their parents and arranged for plane fare back home. They found, by comparison, that home was not as lonely as the City by the Bay.

Jim wrote to me for about a year after this adventure. He eventually met a gay classmate and was determined to make a go of it in his hometown on the East Coast.

Just when I thought that no new problem could arise, the phone rang and I was faced with another unusual and challenging situation.

Brendan was a bright personable freshman at San Francisco State. He was 19 and had been out of the closet for four years. His parents were divorced and his father remarried about six months before he called me. His new stepmother had come into the marriage with two sons, Billy and Tom. As part of the divorce arrangement Brendan's father was given custody of him and a younger sister. Everything was going well in the new family except with 15-year-old Billy, the eldest of his new siblings. Billy and Brendan shared the same room but had separate beds. The problem was that the boy was coming on to Brendan who was having more and more difficulty resisting his overtures. He was attracted to Billy but didn't want to be the cause of a rift in the family. His stepmother believed that gays preyed on boys in order to convert them to their lifestyle. Brendan did not want to validate that prejudice.

Brendan and I met with the father who had noticed a mutual attraction between the two boys but dismissed it as boyish horseplay. The father was understanding and cooperative. He was open to my recommendation to allow Brendan to live in the school dorm or in a room near the campus. Billy visited at least once a week, but Brendan always made sure that someone else was present.

I kept in touch with Brendan until he graduated. By then Billy had developed his own set of friends and was not dependent on Brendan for relationships.

Rarely did I pick up a call from a person saying, "I know someone who needs your help. Here is his phone number." This one was different. A grandmother was calling about a grandchild. She believed her grandchild was threatening suicide. I agreed to go to her home and meet with them. The home was located in Forest Hill, one of the loveliest districts in San Francisco. It was large and attractively furnished. The grandfather was sitting in a lounge chair near the fireplace. He suffered from Alzheimer's disease and was oblivious to my presence. The grandmother introduced me to her grandson, Paul/Pauline. He was sixteen, but looked much younger. He appeared more feminine than masculine. He spoke with a soft, pleasant voice. He told his story frankly and without embarrassment. Paul was born a hermaphrodite, with predominantly male organs. Since his parents already had a daughter, they thought it would be nice to have a son. They instructed the doctor to perform the necessary surgery.

As he developed, it became obvious that Paul was actually more feminine than masculine. This was not a problem in his early years. When he reached adolescence though, he suffered abusive treatment from his peers. The gym shower room was an embarrassing torment for him. He was often beaten after school hours and called names like "fag" and "queer." Paul knew he was not a homosexual. He knew that something was wrong, but he couldn't identify what it was. Though his mother was sympathetic she had no understanding of what was happening to her son. The father simply turned his back on the situation and walked away from the family. At home alone, he would dress in his sister's clothes and use her makeup. He showed me a picture of himself in his sister's prom dress. He looked beautiful.

Paul hated being considered gay. Some of his friendships came to a shattering end when the friend would proposition him. He wasn't interested in sex with a boy anymore than he was with a girl. His sexual expression lived only in his fantasies.

Paul asked questions I was incapable of answering. He wanted to have the initial surgery reversed. I did not know if this was a possibility. I referred him to the hospital where he had been born. He followed up on my suggestion and made an appointment with the physician who had delivered him. The doctor was understanding. Although he was advised that it was possible to reverse the original surgery, in the end, Paul decided not to do this. He continued to need all the support and acceptance he could get. He wanted to continue our counseling sessions, primarily because I did not ridicule him, or consider him gay. I accepted him for who he was and was willing to support him in whatever choice he made.

I called him about a year after our initial meeting. He seemed adjusted and sounded happy. He became more accepting of his situation especially through the help of a support group at a reputable hospital south of San Francisco noted for it a work with transgendered persons.

The problems of the gay community were diverse and complicated. They included not only sexual problems, but emotional and social difficulties as well. In many ways, their problems were no different from those experienced in the straight world. Adjusting to family and social pressures made life difficult for many. Most Church denominations were insensitive to the needs of this community. Many still wrestle with the problem of ordination of openly gay pastors and lay workers. The first mainline denomination to ordain identified gays was the United Church of Christ. But this continues to be a divisive issue in that denomination to the extent that some local churches have withdrawn. Debate continues in other major old-line denominations.

CHAPTER 5

Lonely Sits the City

How lonely sits the city that was full of people!
How like a widow she has become...

—Lamentations 1:1

Loneliness doesn't have to be profound to be destructive. One night I walked into Sam's HofBrau for something to eat. It was crowded so I sat at one of the long community tables across from a man who, during the course of the meal, began to cry. I asked if I could help or if he would like to talk about what was bothering him. My inquiry only caused a greater flood of tears. He was in his mid-thirties, well-dressed and was not drinking. Through his tears he said, "Today is my birthday and there is no one around to wish me a Happy Birthday!"

In view of the tragedy I encountered every night, the simplicity of the problem seemed almost ludicrous, but to experience this kind of isolation from a loving support system can be devastating. I walked him back to his apartment. We continued to see or talk to each other by phone several times during the next months. In one of our last conversations he said, "Just knowing that I can call someone who will listen and who understands, makes life easier."

The ancient Hebrews created a poetic art form called a dirge that through the year experienced a metamorphosis. It moved from a simple funeral spell to keep the dead in their place to a genuine expression of grief over the loss of a loved one. The writers of the book of Lamentations progressed from describing their own personal misfortune and calamities to those of the entire community. What concerned them most was the tragedy that afflicted the lives of those about them. Then, as now, few words are more dreadful to the human mind than "death" and "loneliness." When we consider the emotions generated by these words, we discover a relationship. Loneliness occurs when a person's fear of his or her own death coincides with the death of loved ones. The finality of death and the separation that surrounds it are obvious and so ingrained in our psyche that definitions and explanations are experiential rather than intellectual.

Loneliness also overwhelms us when we feel disconnected. Most of us experience this at one time or another, but we all have difficulty in defining it because of the power of the surrounding emotions. Paul Tillich, in his book *The Eternal Now*, describes two sides of loneliness. He defines "solitude" as the glory of being alone and describes "loneliness" as an expression of the pain of being alone.

Solitude was not a concern for the Night Ministry. Solitude is creative and often sought after, but loneliness can lead to depression and even suicide. It is widespread, affecting not only the nervous, the withdrawn, or the psychotic. In some ways it is a result of the spirit of our age.

There was a time when America was more rural than it was urban. People lived on the land, or in small towns servicing those farming people. People knew each other and were concerned about each other's well being. People grew up, went to school, got married, had children, lived and died not only in the same town, but often in the same house in which they were born. The family and the stability of the marital bond gave a framework to the individual's life. A community of like ideas bound them to the society of which they were a part.

In contrast, today men and women are lost in the anonymity of the large city and of big business. Now, a high percentage of marriages end in divorce and people move or change jobs frequently over the course of their lifetimes. Both factors contribute to loneliness, and its effect on children can be devastating.

It is difficult for those of another generation to really understand or empathize with the loneliness of teenagers of the 1960s and '70s. They lived in an emotional, psychological and physical world so different from the world that their parents experienced. Loneliness was more evident in the cities. The

Loneliness was the most destructive disease night people suffered and shared.

largest group migrating to the City was no longer gathered into community by nationality or race, but by the fact that they were single. These young, single adults, along with older men and women (widowed and retired) make singleness a substantial part of the urban scene. This was especially true of the inner city. Youth were left alone to make the most perilous of intellectual experiments, that of developing their own philosophy of life, without the support of family, the community, or the Church. These single persons were victims of a confusion seldom experienced before in history. They felt themselves alone and lonely.

Initially, the sense of freedom that comes from moving away from family and community seemed exciting and liberating, but developing a support system among strangers was always more difficult than anticipated. Soon the freedom turned to isolation and the isolation to loneliness.

A large contributing factor to this "loneliness of the city" was youth and inexperience. Many of these young migrants were ill-equipped to deal with life alone. They were separated from familiar support systems—family and friends. For the first time they faced the world alone and were caught in the malaise of loneliness. This was a major factor in the growth of the "bar scene" where young singles could go to meet other young singles. Some bars became known for the services they offered: pickup bars for one-night stands, pick-up bars with more long-term plans, cruising bars, and sports bars.

The gay community had a parallel line-up of bars catering to the gays and lesbians migrating to the City. These ranged in appeal from genteel and sophisticated clubs and restaurants, to bars for the tough leather and bike crowd, to places for S&M (an abbreviation for "sadomasochistic" used by both gay and straight crowds seeking expression for their sexual preference). Even small malls and stores had gained a reputation for gay or straight pick-up possibilities. But when a pick-up was not made, going home alone could be devastating.

Shortly after 2:00 a.m. one New Year's Eve, I was walking down Mason Street past The Fantasy Room, a gay bar, which had just closed. From an alley, a bartender I knew called to me. He was trying to support Billy, a very drunk co-worker, who kept slipping down the wall each time he was lifted to his feet. My friend had a date waiting for him in his apartment. Would I get Billy home? Billy could not walk to my car, so I hailed a taxi. I struggled to get this very inebriated young man into his apartment. Fortunately for me, it was on the first floor. All along the way he warned me about his dog. He kept mumbling, "Be careful when you open the door." I envisioned a huge mastiff pouncing on me and tearing at my throat for manhandling his master. When I cautiously opened the door, I was greeted by an almost invisible, prissy-pink, miniature poodle! I got Billy to his bed, slipped off his shoes and started to leave. Before I reached the door I was startled by a shrieking wail. "Here it is New Year's Eve. Everyone's going home with a date and I'm ending up with a PRIEST!"

Billy's problem of loneliness was a common one not only in the gay world, but the straight one as well. Loneliness cannot be drowned in alcohol or relieved by sex. The lonely from both worlds search for partners in specialized establishments. They frequent bars or bathhouses. There the danger from entrapment was diminished. The frustration from unfulfilled desire was so exhausting that the search itself provided an escape from loneliness. The found partner provided relief for an hour or even a night. Then the search resumed and became compulsive.

Some persons found erotic companionship more appealing and more human than resignation to loneliness. Others felt that touching another may be more intimate and more honest than watching. No one can really find his or her own identity in another, least of all in the body of another. This misinterpretation of the meaning of sex often leads to possessiveness, a cannibalism that devours the very object of love.

In a city like San Francisco, there were not only migrants from other parts of the country, but an influx of teenagers from Mexico and Central and South America. While working along Polk Street, I came across four young men from Central America. Each night I found them huddled together in a doorway or aimlessly wandering the streets. One spoke a little English. At first they were afraid of me and would have nothing to do with me, partly because I was a "priest" and partly because I was an adult authority figure. But after weeks of seeing me, and realizing that I made no effort to counsel or hassle them, they began to open up.

All four were undocumented. All had jobs in a restaurant and could afford a place to stay, though they chose not to spend money for housing. They ate at the restaurant where they worked, and were well fed. All (two were brothers) sent the bulk of their earnings back home to help support their families in Central America. Their dream was to earn enough to be able to bring their families north. They were terrified of being discovered and sent home. They were living in a city more than a hundred times larger then their small home village. They were isolated and antagonized, even by other Spanish-speaking street people. These four young boys, barely into their teens, were paranoid, enormously lonely, and depressed. As their trust in me grew I was able to connect them with an agency that offered safe surroundings and English courses that nurtured and protected them. It encouraged and gave them some glimmer of hope, helped them work through and deal with their loneliness and isolation.

During my twelve years in the Night Ministry, I processed hundreds of calls from those suffering from acute loneliness, chronic illness, or infirmity. Widows and widowers, forgotten by both family and friends, often felt like "fifth wheels" among their peers. After the death of a partner, visits or invitations from friends became less frequent until at last they were left alone with no physical contact with anyone except an occasional delivery person. Many times someone would be referred to me by a Greyhound bus dispatcher or telephone operator dialed by a lonely stranger desperate just to hear another human voice.

Almost every night I met loneliness in a more intense way than I had ever experienced before. A young serviceman from Montana, still in his teens, on his way overseas in the era of the Vietnam war, was frightened by the fear of death and lonely because he had been thrust into a life-style unfamiliar and alien. Elderly men and women, unable to sleep and depressed by the dinginess of the rooms in which they lived, walked the streets during the dark hours of the night or sat in all-night restaurants in the hopes of finding someone with whom to visit.

An elderly widow called me regularly. She was going blind and was frightened, as anyone would be. She lived alone in a small apartment she and her late husband had first rented some thirty-five years earlier. She had no family and was the last of her generation of friends still alive. Her investment income was no longer adequate to pay all her expenses and the fear of being destitute was overpowering. Suicide seemed to be the answer. I was able to negotiate with her sympathetic and understanding apartment manager. She moved into a smaller apartment. The cost was less. A volunteer caregiver stopped by once a week to help her shop and do her chores. She also signed up for "Meals On Wheels." These steps helped to meet her physical needs.

How does one cope with the kind of desolation brought on by alcoholism? How does one deal with the loneliness of the person who has effectively driven his or her family and friends away? Are these people to be forgotten when they struggle in the middle of the night against demons that can destroy them? Sometimes it is impossible to keep those who are determined to kill themselves from doing so. More often, a bit of human warmth and understanding at the right moment can pull someone back from the brink. Then steps can be taken to give that person the opportunity to recover from the isolation of the moment.

The night brought me in contact with all segments of society, from the wealthy to the destitute, from the pietistic to the prostitute. I talked to performers and strippers and gays, all with one element in common: an oppressive loneliness, which they attempted to mask with drugs and alcohol. They felt isolated, separated, and deserted by both "respectable" society, as well as by the Church. Now, for the first time in their lives, at least, the Church was creative, and not judgmental, meeting them within the framework of their own experience.

It was good for me to be reminded that Jesus faced the risk of meeting people in their own element along the dirty and dismal streets of His time and often at their convenience and not His. When Nicodemus wanted to talk to Jesus, he didn't choose a respectable office hour, but "came to Jesus by night." There were those who needed the seclusion and protection of night to face both themselves and their troubles, and the Church was there.

God wisely created us to live in fellowship with each other and, although we sometimes forget it, we have a responsibility to each other. I cannot love God without loving my brother and sister, no matter how lowly, destitute, or unsavory he or she may appear. We must be ready to serve God in that moment, even though it may be at an inconvenient hour. As acclaimed Secretary-General of the United Nations Dag Hammarskjold put it: "Pray that your loneliness may spur you into finding something to live for, great enough to die for."

CHAPTER 6

To Be or Not

D o we just forget that person for whom all the burdens, all the problems, all the tragedies, bearable by daylight, overwhelm him at night until there seems to be no answer, no hope, no way out except in suicide? Who is there to hear? And when there is someone to hear, what is there to say?

Working with the suicidal person can be extremely difficult on the one hand and precariously easy on the other. It is difficult because one is working with a suffering person in the depths of his or her despondency. It is easy because, in most instances, he or she is looking for an alternative, for a way out. It was the task of the Night Ministry to suggest or provide that alternative.

Some of the reasons people consider suicide may leave you with the feeling that they can't really be serious, that the problem is too mundane to be taken as a genuine threat. But such is not the case! The simplest problem can be the pebble, which sets off a landslide leading to eventual death.

A first year student in a Roman Catholic seminary in the Bay Area arranged to spend a few nights with me on the street. He had a tenseness about him, which made me suspect a hidden agenda that he wanted to share but didn't know how. Near the end of our third night together he quietly and calmly told me that he was contemplating suicide. He loved the Church. His old parish priest was a beloved friend of the family and a good role model, but he was sure he could never live up to his priest's or his parents' or his own expectations. "And anyway, I'm not good enough!" He blurted out that no matter how hard he tried not to, and no matter how hard he prayed, he still had "immoral thoughts" and masturbated several times a week. He had difficulty making friends in spite of his Irish good looks and bright smile. He was certain he was a "pervert" with no control over his sexuality and would be a danger to any parish he served.

He had a clumsy, adolescent sexual experience when he was sixteen and still felt tremendous guilt. We talked for several hours that night and I met with him in person or talked with him by phone for several months. Eventually, I introduced him to a priest who I knew would be sympathetic to his struggle, a man who could help the young seminarian come to terms with his sexuality in the context of his Catholic beliefs. During one of my last visits he said he was no longer thinking about suicide and had decided not to leave the seminary.

Teen suicide was an increasing tragedy during my time with the Night Ministry experience and it was particularly prevalent among gay teenagers. I believe that many of the deaths of teenagers, both straight and gay, were more accidental than intentional. They experimented with drugs to see how far they could go, how high they could get. They "played" with suicidal tools like ropes, guns, and knives. Sometimes they cut off their oxygen supply while masturbating in order to enhance their orgasm. Often these deaths appeared to be suicides but were really experiments that got out of control.

Do we really understand the loneliness of the teenager, living in an emotional, psychological, and physical world so different from the world in which most of us grew up? More and more children are being raised in single-parent homes. The daily contact with that parent is often frantic and spasmodic. Sometimes a parent's boyfriend or girlfriend will enter the household, and rather than creating a family, the friend will have no interest in the children of the new spouse. Running away or being pushed away from the home is often the result. Can we understand the feeling of a young teenager who realizes that he or she is gay and is thrown out of the home by an unsympathetic parent? Or the young girl who is abused by her father and other family members and who thinks she has no recourse except the streets? Many kids are kicked

One last word before he
makes up his mind whether
to live or die.

out of their homes because of economic reasons. They have reached sixteen, and are "old enough to work." So they are pushed out on the streets to make room for younger siblings. Have you ever considered the stress and danger these adolescents experience on the streets? They experience the stress of not knowing whether they will eat that day or not. There is always the danger of being picked up by a "john" who may be psychotic and do them harm—and add to all that the stress and danger of catching a disease!

Often a life-threatening suicide attempt would be made just before a friend or family member was expected home. If the expected person was delayed for some reason, or if the anticipated rescue did not come, the attempt resulted in death, even though the person did not intend to take his or her life.

Jason came to the Night Ministry through Trinity Episcopal Church. He was a faithful and competent volunteer. Gay and handicapped, he suffered prejudice and rejection by his family and the larger society. Born into a privileged and cultured family, he arrived "at the wrong time" as far as his mother was concerned. She was at the height of her musical career. Taking time off to raise a child would not advance that career. Later, as a youth, Jason developed polio which left his left side paralyzed. During his teens, the realization of his homosexuality was the last straw for his mother. He was sent to a boarding school and never returned home.

At Christmas time, my wife and I entertained the Night Ministry board members and volunteers at an open house. Jason was the first to arrive and the last to leave.

Later that night, he called to say how much he enjoyed being in a regular home again. He said he called his mother, asking if he could come home to celebrate Christmas with his family. She refused, "Maybe next year." He told me it didn't matter, "Everything will be all right." He then drank a bottle of wine and swallowed a number of Nembutals. He was found dead the next morning.

Rick called me with threats of suicide. He had moved to San Francisco from one of the cities on the Gulf. His Greek immigrant father owned a small fleet of shrimp boats. Rick was gay, but had been "in the closet" to his conservative Greek Orthodox parents. He returned to Mississippi for the funeral of his grandmother. While there, he decided to tell his parents of his homosexuality. They had been a close, loving, and supportive family, but homosexuality was something they would not tolerate. He was told to go back to San Francisco and never return home again. His parents did not want him to "contaminate" his younger brothers. He was devastated and saw no solution but suicide.

I steered him to Glide Memorial Church that had a creative outreach program for the people of the Tenderloin in which he became involved. The church community welcomed and helped him regain some self-esteem. His father eventually welcomed him back into the family circle. We remained friends for five years after the initial contact.

Society has been so harsh on gays that even the two institutions that should be most supportive and loving, the family and churches, sometimes condemn them. The rejection is so complete that death seems to be the only way out. Parents feel "betrayed" by sons and daughters who have "chosen" to do this to them. The parents feel guilty and blame each other for the homosexuality of their child. A once perfectly good marriage sometimes ends up in divorce, leaving the gay child with an additional guilt trip.

Rick's story was not unique. In fact, it was repeated again and again. It covered the spectrum of ages from sixteen-year-old Billy to a fifty-six-year-old ex-priest. Billy was from the East Bay. His mother and stepfather kicked him out of their home because they didn't want this "sick, disgusting kid living in their house, contaminating the neighbors' children." They felt disgraced. The ex-priest was defrocked when his homosexuality became public. The church made no effort to love and accept him, but simply condemned him. Protestants were just as reproachful and condemning.

Ray was a man in his early fifties, balding, rotund, and very dirty! He invited me to his room in one of the ubiquitous cheap resident hotels on O'Farrell Street in the Tenderloin. I saw him often on the streets but had little conversation with him. His room crawled with roaches, and was stifling, but Ray would not allow the windows to be opened because "they" would come in. "They" were crawly little monsters who were after him. Ray had been a priest but had been defrocked because of his alcoholism and his persistent homosexual activity with several youths in his parish. What made things worse was that his younger brother was also a priest, and a very success-ful one. Sibling rivalry, gayness, and alcoholism (I never saw him sober) all contributed to a depression almost impossible to penetrate. Our relationship continued for several years. His condition never improved. This was primarily because he refused to take any responsibility for his condition or steps toward rehabilitation. The Catholic Diocese did offer help: counseling, and care at a retreat center. Eventually Ray disappeared from the streets. He was one of my "regulars" who vanished without a trace.

It was not unusual for me to get a call from someone whose world seemed to be collapsing. Some calls were from faithful parishioners who didn't want to bother their pastor or priest. Instead, they turned to a stranger for counsel. More tragic was the call from the faithful, or even not so faithful, parishioner, who in desperation had tried to call the pastor or priest and had been met by no answer, or even worse, an impersonal, overly protective answering service which refused to put the call through. This rejection was sometimes more than the caller could tolerate; so he or she found an answer in death. Although there were agencies available to help guide some troubled persons toward a solution to their problem, referral was a dangerous tool if offered too quickly in the course of counseling. For many, "referral" is just another name for "rejection."

Many who called the Night Ministry demanded anonymity. Soon they would see for themselves that this was not just another game being played in a world of games, and so offered a name, an address, and eventually, requested a visit. For some, the telephone was a monstrous, impersonal machine, symbolic of a monstrous, impersonal world; they insisted on a personal visit.

Although, obviously, a visit was initially more time-consuming than a telephone call, it also allowed for much more creative counseling in a shorter period of time. Counseling by telephone made it difficult to evaluate the urgency of a caller. It was more difficult to determine whether it was a real cry for help or just a bid for attention. Although "a cry for help" was indicative of more sinister problems, it usually was not at least immediately life threatening and a response could be postponed until a less hectic time in the life of the caller. I was surprised when a hysterical, suicidal person called and said, as one did when he found I was busy with another suicidal person, "O.K., finish with the person you are with now, but listen as fast as you can and call me as soon as you're available."

For some, the phone was enough of a link to dissuade them from any drastic action, at least for that moment. But for many, the impersonal telephone only exaggerated the sense of isolation and aloneness. A personal contact had to be made. Someone not only had to listen; someone had to go!

Jack called from a flophouse south of the Slot (a name given to the area south of Market Street when cable cars were hauled along by cables under the street, through a slot between the tracks). When I got there I found a middle-aged man sitting on the edge of a dirty, but unslept-in bed. He was aimlessly playing with a 38-caliber revolver. The world he knew and loved was gone.

Jack and his wife had been managers of a small, inexpensive, residential hotel. Part of the salary package had been the free use of one of the rental units. He and his wife and two-year-old son had lived there, not elegantly but comfortably. On Easter day several months before he called, his wife was preparing an Easter dinner for several of the older and more indigent residents. She needed one more ingredient so Jack ran down to the neighborhood grocery store to pick it up. When he returned a brief time later, he walked into an unbelievably gruesome scene. His wife had been savagely beaten to death, and his little son was so brutalized that he was left brain-damaged without hope of recovery. The rent receipts were missing. The murderer had not been found.

The only escape he could think of from the guilt he felt for not being there for his family when they needed him most, and the overwhelming loneliness he experienced in their loss, was death. But something in the back of his mind unconsciously was seeking an alternative, so he made one final call to the Night Ministry. Here was a man in deep depression, needing serious professional help. I risked suggesting a referral. Jack agreed to my calling a psychiatrist friend interning at San Francisco General Hospital. As I dialed the number I uttered a silent prayer that he would be on duty. Fortunately he was. Within an hour Jack was examined, processed and hospitalized. Several years later, after his recovery, Jack called me to tell me that he had happily remarried and his new wife was pregnant. Unfortunately, the son who had been beaten would be hospitalized for the remainder of his life.

Another time, I was called by a hysterical woman. She was living in a beautiful apartment on Russian Hill. The apartment was more like a movie set than a comfortable home. Persian rugs covered the floors, beautiful original art work hung on the walls; the den furniture was upholstered in zebra skins, and dramatic lighting emphasized her good taste (though not her sense of conservation). She was surrounded by all the obvious and external comforts a person could want. But something was missing. Her marriage was falling apart and, for her, the collapse of the marriage was the collapse of her life. She woke up after a few hours of restless sleep overwhelmed by the terrible loneliness felt only by those who have been betrayed by someone they trusted and loved. She was alone in the apartment, knew her husband was with another woman, and considered killing herself. She called Suicide Prevention instead, and was referred to me. After hours of counseling over a period of several weeks, she stabilized. I also met regularly with the husband. They decided to consult with their Rabbi and eventually reaffirm their marriage vows. A year after I was called to the woman's home, I met her at a reception at the De Young Museum, but she claimed she had never met me before. It was common for callers to want to deny that they had shared their most intimate problems with a stranger.

Coincidentally, that same night I received a similar call from a woman living in a cheap residential hotel on Turk Street. Her surroundings were just the opposite of the woman's on Russian Hill. This studio apartment was furnished with cheap, mass-produced furniture and the pictures on the walls were inexpensive reproductions. But the pain she felt, the sense of betrayal she experienced, was just as real and just as debilitating as that felt by the woman who was surrounded by an abundance of worldly possessions.

A call came through Suicide Prevention from a woman in her sixties threatening to take her life. She had several failed suicide attempts behind her, but who can predict whether the next might not be successful? We talked for hours about her dead husband, about her drinking problem stimulated by loneliness, about her son who gave up on her and didn't seem to care any more. Over a period of time she was able to purge herself of some guilt, rid herself of animosity and resentment, and eventually said those words the crisis counselor works so hard to hear: "I think you've helped me find a reason to live."

Many times I received calls from someone newly divorced who would say, "Oh, I'm not suicidal or anything like that. It's just that when I woke up the bed felt so empty." Separation can be just as devastating and sometimes more traumatic than the death of a loved one.

CHAPTER 7

Who Are These Kids Anyway?

Letisha, a skinny young prostitute, her lacquered bouffant wig incongruously in place in spite of the pounding rain, stopped me and said, "Bless me, Father. Business is bad!" We visited for a while but I didn't stay too long. I didn't want to get her into trouble with her pimp who kept circling the block in his vintage Cadillac, giving both of us dirty looks.

Over time I learned that she had been sexually molested by her father and two older brothers. "At least now I'm getting paid for it," she said. She was sixteen years old. Her only happiness was the prospect of another fix. I saw her regularly but only for brief and passing conversations. These encounters were enough, though, to help build some sense of worth and self-esteem.

Because of the loneliness, fear, isolation or crisis often felt in the Tenderloin and Polk Gulch, initial contact with the young people in those areas was not difficult. They were anxious and ready to talk to an adult they could trust and who they felt understood them. But because these cruising areas were in constant flux, follow-up was often impossible or at best, difficult. Admittedly, the situations I encountered were usually extreme and certainly not characteristic of the general population of youth of a comparable age. Nevertheless, looking at this microcosm of the population, I anticipated that their actions foretold a trend likely to spread to other cities and to young people other than runaways.

In general, the Tenderloin/Polk Gulch young adults lived by rules made up along the way. They had broken away from structure, from families, from the establishment, and struck out on their own. This "breaking away" had not been a life pattern since the Great Depression. Then youths left home for financial reasons. These young people left behind the guidelines and standards, which had given other generations a framework within which to function. As they moved (either by choice or circumstance) from childhood into adulthood, they lost out on adolescence. There was no rite of passage, no earning of one's own name, no symbolic hunt that moved him or her from boyhood or girlhood to adulthood. Instead, they were left to grope and struggle by themselves in order to discover, sometimes in isolation, their own identity.

In some areas of our country, and particularly within certain ethnic communities, the male/female role was still clearly defined. Young people from these backgrounds, coming from structured surroundings to the streets, experienced culture shock. Roles were no longer defined and neither were the rules, so the search for identity became more and more confused. Spiritual identity is usually the first to be abandoned, followed by family ties. As they become more and more enmeshed in a variety of sexual expressions not known to them and not available to them in other circumstances, sexual identity becomes blurred.

Tommy and Hank were brothers from a farm in central Kansas. Their home was just a few miles from my first parish. They had a strong Mennonite religious background. Both boys resented the strict teaching of their faith. Hank was the more restless of the two. He decided to respond to the lure of the West and travel to San Francisco.

His room back in Kansas was covered with psychedelic posters. His parents hated the posters because they considered them incompatible with their faith teachings. This controversy only served to fuel his desire to leave home. He had experimented with marijuana. Now he was eager to try something else. Hank had been sexually active with a girl in his high school class for two years. He wanted "more action with more women." He considered himself too young to settle down with just one.

Tommy was thirteen, and not as experienced as Hank. He did share some of his older brother's restlessness. He was a sweet, rather innocent kid. He had not used any drugs, and was still a virgin. Hank had tried to tempt Tommy with marijuana. He also teased him about a neighbor girl. Hank said she had the "hots" for Tommy. Tommy pestered his brother until Hank agreed to take him along to San Francisco. The parents disapproved but caved under the constant pressure applied by both boys. On the day they left Kansas, their father slipped one hundred dollars to each of the boys to help them on their way.

I met the two boys while listening to a rock and roll group performing on the West end of the Panhandle. The boys were surprised to see a "priest" in the crowd. They approached me rather than the other way around. They told me their story like a couple of performers relating their journey with a little pride in what they had accomplished.

There were scores of hippie types traveling the same direction. Marijuana was abundant. This was not the action Tommy was seeking. He was not interested in pot. All that was on his mind was to lose his virginity. This would not be difficult for a good-looking husky farm boy. But it didn't happen as he dreamed it would. The sexual freedom the two boys experienced was strange, even for San Francisco. Hank would have Tommy stay in the bedroom while he was having sex so, "he could see how it was done." When Hank finished, he allowed Tommy to take over. This was not how Tommy fantasized he would have his first sexual experience. However, stimulated by the visual scene of watching his brother, he did experience physical pleasure. His first sex act was not as exciting as Tommy dreamed it would be.

I counseled both of them about what they were doing. I advised Hank that what he was doing with Tommy could be considered child abuse and molestation. I also warned him of the implications these actions had on his own sexuality. Their strong religious upbringing began to surface. Despite the fact that Tommy was enjoying his new sexual life, he exclaimed, "Mom would be disappointed in us if she knew what we are doing."

Hank continued to use marijuana, but never experimented with anything harder. Tommy's sex life became more private.

I ran into the two boys regularly on Haight Street. They seemed to adjust to the scene. They were always glad to see me and join me for coffee in the Drogstore. After about a year, they decided to return to Kansas. I never heard from them again.

The most difficult thing for me about the Night Ministry was the lack of closure. I would be so intimately involved in people's lives then, suddenly, they would disappear, never to be heard from again.

I have been able to keep in touch on a continuing basis with only one person from the thousands I met in San Francisco. We have written or called each other regularly for more than thirty years. He has had an impact on my life. I watched him grow from boyhood into manhood, saw him become a successful businessman and a caring and loving father. When I first met him I knew his quest was more than most of the kids I met on the street. His was a spiritual journey that eventually found a home in a gathered support community called the Church. If his was the only life I helped to change in the Night Ministry then all twelve years were worthwhile.

Despite the fact that most of these kids were street wise, there was still considerable confusion about the status or rules regulating physical intimacy between the sexes. Historically there had always been sexual interchange between both adults and adolescents. The difference today is that what was once considered promiscuity is now considered normal. People are no longer caught up in Victorian taboos practiced by previous generations. The present problem was less one of rebelling against one's parents, and more of losing one's self in a lifestyle with unknown limits.

It was popular for parents and sociologists to feel that the best approach in dealing with the sexual revolution affecting the younger generation was to let each individual decide what was best for himself.

The fact that those street kids accepted their actions as being normal is what set them apart from past generations. They felt they did not need boundaries.

Signing up for a crash pad at Hospitality House, a shelter for adolescents.

The "deciding what is best for himself" (or herself) is the point at which I saw most of the street kids floundering. They didn't know what they wanted or even what they didn't want. Their new found freedom demanded a rejection of past guidelines and therefore a rejection of what they at least unconsciously wanted. No longer could the family, the indissolubility of the marital bonds, the security of jobs in the city or the cohesiveness of the village give a framework to the individual's life, a community of common ideas. It left them feeling alone and lost.

In addition, the unbelievably rapid technological advances, space travel, moon walks, organ transplants, speed of communication and more, meant the loss of the awe and wonder of a new frontier at a younger and younger age. Blasé, sophisticated youth lost their pioneering spirit of adventure. There seemed to be no more frontiers.

Being deprived of structure and goals left these young people more confused and in a more desolate adolescent wasteland than that experienced by earlier teenagers for whom there had been a thread of similarity and continuity running through the generations. The young people I dealt with could not relate to the hero-myths of past generations (this was before "Star Wars"), and the dreams they dreamed were often those stimulated by consciousness-altering drugs.

When our economy moved from rural to urban, our young people found themselves lost in the anonymity of the city and of big business. They were left alone to make the most perilous of intellectual experiments—that of developing their own philosophies of life. They were the unwitting participants in a confusion never before known in history. Is it any wonder they felt themselves to be without identity?

Some people felt that that state was not all negative. Sociologist David Mace has pointed out that, in looking at all the confusion about the identity of the roles of men and women in our contemporary culture, it would appear on the surface that our kids are in turmoil. He felt that there was a new opportunity to discover new roles in both sexes.

It is virtually impossible to separate a youth's sexual inclinations and practices from the innumerable influences bombarding his or her life on a variety of levels. Being aware of some of these influences and their effects can be of considerable value in understanding the street relationships of young men and women.

The Women's Liberation Movement was doing an excellent job of raising the consciousness of women and men alike, but not without some negative consequences. The young male who was raised in a traditional family where the roles of mother and father were traditional and clearly defined was often left confused and threatened by the unfamiliar self-assertiveness of his female contemporaries. As women gained in power and status, he felt as though he had lost some of his power and status, so confusion about his role set in. The thought of female competition in areas heretofore reserved for men was often more than his psyche could tolerate. When he came to the realization that his girlfriend didn't need him, that she could get along just as well, if not better, without him, he was left impotent or psychologically castrated. But while that male who still believed that a woman's role is "Kinder, Küche, Kirche" (Children, Kitchen, Church) may preserve much of his male ego, he lost a great deal in human relationships.

For the first time in history, the female could hold the key to her own pregnancy. Until the discovery of "The Pill," contraception was almost totally male oriented and it was the male who decided on the quality or the use of a contraceptive device.

In many of the world's cultures, a woman who knew herself to be fertile felt more feminine, more attractive, more desirable. The man also found her to be more attractive, consciously or unconsciously, a prospect for the demonstration of his virility via impregnation. With a young man just venturing into the new world of sex, impotence could develop when his partner insisted on the use of some form of contraception. With others, getting at least one partner pregnant was important in order to demonstrate and prove their masculinity. The thought of responsibility toward the child, however, was seldom considered.

Along with the Pill came another facet of sexuality never suspected by males: women could enjoy sex too! In fact, they may enjoy it to the extent of initiating the sex act. These young men found that the streetwalkers with whom they mingled weren't at all like the girls in their sophomore high school class back in rural Iowa. The self-assertiveness of some young women, their insistence on more sex, on how and when they wanted it, was a threat to young males who felt that the initiative should be entirely theirs.

The very young people, fifteen to seventeen, coming into the Tenderloin were totally absorbed by the discovery of sex and they liked it. They became so preoccupied with the mere mechanics of sex that they had little awareness of the depth of their own sexual feelings. But as the newness of sexual experimentation wore off, questions about their sexual identity began to arise. The openness with which many of these teenagers talked about the most intimate aspects of their relationships continued to surprise me. The boys were the most eager to talk about their sexuality, especially if they were in a small group of the same age. The girls were a little more hesitant, but once they found that I was trying to be helpful and not judgmental, they were as open as the boys. For many I became a father figure.

None of these children enjoyed the comfort of living in a "Father Knows Best" family. Many didn't have fathers, or they had fathers who wouldn't talk to them about intimate aspects of their lives. One of the things that worried the boys was noticing that they didn't get turned on as quickly or as often as when they first entered the world of sex. They became frightened at first, convinced that their masculinity was at stake whenever they found that they couldn't "bone" whenever or whomever they pleased. Their sexuality threatened, they would talk to anyone they could trust.

As my reputation became more secure on the streets, an increasing number of them turned to me, not so much for help but more for advice and as someone to whom they could vent. As these boys became more discriminating in choosing sex partners they gradually became aware of a host of other emotions involved in the act they came to call "making love."

It was my experience in working with young Tenderloin males that many were indifferent about the use of the Pill when being promiscuous. They felt that the Pill was a woman's prerogative and responsibility. If she got pregnant, that was her problem, not theirs. It never occurred to them that prevention of pregnancy was a mutual responsibility. But when one found an "old lady" and settled down, this responsibility became his also.

At the outset of my work with street kids, I found an almost unanimous objection to the use of condoms. Almost all young males complained they were too small. Another objection was the perceived loss of sensation and spontaneity. Another was what they considered a loss of eroticism when they could not ejaculate in their partners. This was not only a male phenomenon; many young women felt the same way. This negative attitude toward condoms changed drastically with the onslaught of AIDS, which entered the scope of the Night Ministry during the 1980s. The condom was no longer used only for birth control; it could be a lifesaver. One of the important tasks I performed was to distribute condoms to street kids, straight or gay. Later, sterile syringes and needles were also passed out on the street. This was illegal, but the police simply looked the other way, knowing this was an antidote to the syringes and hypodermic needles that were being used communally to inject a variety of drugs—a perfect way to spread disease.

As far as I was able to determine, no single word among youth described sexual activity with a number of partners, often at the same time. A generation before, "swinging" had described this kind of conduct. The early adolescent involved in group sex with those several years older faced myriad problems and threats to his or her identity.

Alcohol and other drugs lowered inhibitions, causing subliminal doubts to surface. The very young male, sexually inexperienced, wondered about his "performance." He needed constant reassurance and asked his partner again and again, "Was I good? Was it good for you?" Premature ejaculation made him feel inadequate and not as masculine as his older friends who had more experience and more control. Penile size often brought on anxiety for the young male who compared himself to his older friends who were "better hung."

Young girls, too, perceived themselves as inadequate when they found their boyfriends turned on by the more voluptuous bodies of their older friends. For the young male especially, misunderstood homosexual feelings brought on trauma and confusion. In the heat of passion in the midst of a number of naked intertwined bodies, he might find himself turned on by another male, and not understanding the dynamics of his feelings, considered himself "queer." Young adolescent women were often encouraged by their male partners to get involved in lesbian activity while the males watched.

In the areas in which I worked, where sexual freedom was the norm, there was often confusion between the sex act and masculinity/womanhood. The "Stud" syndrome (denoting a well-built, well-hung male always on the make, seeking another sexual conquest) was prevalent for the male and "boning" became a numbers game. The meaning of "womanhood" for the female likewise depended on how many men she seduced. Both confused the accumulation of sex partners with being adult.

I discovered that the socio-economic background of the young individual in formative years had some influence on his or her attitude toward and response to sex. Generally speaking, young persons from rural areas, from "hardhat" families, or from lower income brackets, were more sexually conservative even though they might be sexually more active. They were more inclined to do just "straight" sex with little experimentation. The strict role models set by their parents and older friends exerted positive as well as negative influences on the young people seeking independence. They might develop a creative and positive attitude toward the male/female role, or find that exaggerated parental roles made it impossible to live up to the models. Often, living apart (particularly during early adolescence) from the influence of parents exaggerated their anxiety. They were left alone to decide what it means to be male or female, or worse, to be influenced only by their peers, who were as much adrift as they were.

I do not mean to imply that an adolescent from a more educated home or higher economic bracket had an easier task in discovering his or her identity. The ingredients might be different but the problems were the same. The masculine/feminine role might not be as clearly defined. Often, in more affluent homes, the mother also went off to work in the morning and both parents came home to household tasks. These parents were often more permissive, which the adolescent mistook for lack of concern. The father was often so engrossed in business affairs and the mother so absorbed by social, community, or work commitments, that the child was left without a sense of family support in spite of his or her living in a lovely, comfortable suburban home with several cars in the garage. Life on the street or communal living then gave a sense of support never received in the familial framework.

On the whole, young people in the Tenderloin were not as uptight about homosexuality as those in other parts of the country, although in my seventeen years of working with youth on the streets (comprised of twelve years with the Night Ministry and another five as a volunteer with the Larkin Street Youth

Center), I did see a change in this area of thinking. Ambiguity about sexual partners (especially if they were involved in group sex), sexual experimentation, and the acceptance of oral sex were common. However, those (especially young males) for whom homosexuality was a serious threat were infuriated when a gay hustler made a pass. The obvious, flamboyant gay man turned him off. He could not come to terms with his own homosexual feelings simply because he would not acknowledge that these feelings even existed. The homophobic young person exposed to this lifestyle for the first time might himself be gay, but unaware of it.

Occasionally, for a variety of reasons, including his identity struggle, a young man who was straight would find it easier to relate to the gay community. He might have been a shy person having difficulty in taking the initiative with women. A homosexual friend would take the lead, shifting the responsibility for social contact. The straight youth was now the one being courted. The roles shifted, although his sexual preference did not.

Josh was a tall, muscular, out-of-doors type whose shy personality reminded me of Jimmy Stewart. Born and raised on a ranch in Montana, he had very little social contact. There were seven in his high school graduating class; none were girls. A friend of his older brother, about two years his senior, persuaded him to join him in a move to San Francisco. Moving didn't change Josh's personality. He was still shy and had no idea of how to meet women. To make things worse, his friend was gay. Although he never came on to Josh, his friend was of no help in introducing him to the straight community. Josh started hanging out with gay friends although he didn't get sexually involved with any of them. He found a social life with a few women but without sexual or emotional involvement. It was momentarily satisfying but not emotionally fulfilling.

Many straight teenage young men came into the City and found it difficult to find work. The need for the basic elements of life would lead them to do almost anything to earn enough money to rent a room and buy food. For many male run-a-ways, hustling proved too lucrative to resist. As psychologist Nick Lestardo, director of Larkin Street Youth Services in San Francisco, explained in a Larkin Street newsletter:

> Male hustling is a good way to make $75 to $200 a night. Many of these boys have already been sexually abused. They realize nobody will hire a 15-year-old. They hear, "It's not so horrible." Twenty-five bucks for ten minutes sounds like a lot of money to kids.

It was not unusual for a straight young man to be picked up by a gay, who would pay him for sex. Hustlers would relate some unusual story about their tricks. Often in the middle of the sex act, an older man would say to a young hustler, "You remind me of my son. He's about your age."

Sometimes two or three couples would band together into a "family group" or loosely knit commune. They would alternate in "working" the streets. Sometimes a girl or two would prostitute for the night, and the next night it might be her boyfriend selling his body. They could rationalize that they were doing it just for the money, refusing to admit that they enjoyed the experience.

I also saw a substantial amount of dating between gay males and straight females, who were called "fruit flies." The gay maintained the façade of a heterosexual relationship and the woman didn't have to be concerned about sexual involvement. This, too, changed during my years on the street as Gay Pride and anti-discrimination laws brought more and more gays and lesbians out of the closet. It wasn't any longer necessary to hide behind a pretense of being straight in the work place, although the closet was still necessary when dealing with the family.

Many drifting young people, particularly adolescents, often felt isolated, alone and, in many instances, deserted. Sheer loneliness led to behavior patterns causing identity conflicts. They would be willing to experiment with relationships otherwise avoided during more stable (less lonely) times. The young male, picked up and sometimes supported by an older female, would often have difficulties with his sense of self-worth. The initial feeling of being a "stud" soon diminished when he discovered his loss of freedom and became smothered by her possessiveness.

Loneliness could lead some adolescents into an almost pathological promiscuity. The desire was not so much to accumulate "conquests" as it was to not be alone. Sex became an act devoid of pleasure, resulting in a difficulty in sifting through the emotions that could result in a more significant relationship. Such a young person would eventually lose his or her sexuality and, aside from the act, become almost asexual.

A well-dressed, well-groomed middle-aged man came into the lower bar of the Mark Hopkins Hotel where I was visiting with a friend. With this man was an extremely handsome younger man, also well groomed. He didn't look much older than eighteen, although his ID listed his age as twenty-one. When I got up to leave, the younger man, Chris, followed me and pulled me into a hallway out of sight of the bar. He told me he was straight but was picked up by the older man while he was hustling and was now a "kept boy." He was literally a slave of the older man. He was provided with everything he needed: excellent food, grand parties, and fashionable clothes. This was in exchange for sex on demand. He had everything except freedom. He asked me to help him escape. Before we could formulate a plan, the older man sent a waiter to find us. I expected a call from Chris during the week, but none came.

I went to the Mark the next weekend hoping to see him there again. As I was about to leave, the pair came in. The young man had obviously been beaten. His cheek was swollen and one eye was blackened. The look on his face broke my heart. It wasn't one of anger or rebellion, but of defeat and resignation. Chris eyes dropped as we passed and the older man whispered to me, "Talk to him again and he's dead!" I believed him.

A month or so later I saw them pull up in front of the Mark Hopkins in a BMW. I took down the license number and had a policeman friend check it out. The car belonged to a well-known realtor from Marin County. I never saw the boy or the man again.

This young man, very likely straight as he proclaimed, got involved in hustling primarily out of loneliness and the need for food and housing. He was seduced by the glamour of a beautiful apartment, fine clothes and lavish parties. All this faded when he discovered that the "freedom" he came to San Francisco to enjoy was lost in the slavery of being a "kept" boy. The manhood he wanted to move into when he left home soon disappeared when he surrendered it to a lifestyle completely alien to what he grew up with in his small mid-western town. His good looks, perhaps outstanding in his hometown, were commonplace on the streets of San Francisco.

There is no doubt that such a male hustler was involved in an overt homosexual act even though he might vehemently proclaim his straightness. He may go home with a gay john, spend the night with the sex customer, and may even enjoy the sex act, but insist he is doing it only for the money. A lonely young male may allow himself to be picked up simply because it is better to be warm in bed with someone than it is to go back to a dingy room alone.

Certain behavior patterns usually are a result of circumstances rather than of deliberate choice. These led to serious identity problems among the adolescents with whom I worked and counseled. Ambivalent feelings about their identity resulted from a lack of opportunity to work through the conflict between their feelings and their actions while surrounded by a loving and caring support system. They surrendered their natural maturation process for the "quick fix." They came to San Francisco alone and often left alone, alone with experiences they preferred to forget. Some left with experiences they could never share. Some suffered permanent emotional wounds that left scars that could not be healed without considerable counseling.

CHAPTER 8

Runaways, Throwaways and Pushaways

I went into the Night Ministry thinking I would be working primarily with adults, street-wise people who had been around the block a time or two. I discovered all too quickly and all too painfully that this was not the case.

Mark Twain, in his *Adventures of Huckleberry Finn*, writes about a young teenager, ragged, neglected and motherless, always trying to avoid his drunken father's beatings. When Huck was fourteen, he manages to get away from him, and, "running for his life," meets old Jim, a black slave who also is running for his life. Although our runaways today may resemble Huck and his pal Tom Sawyer in some romantic way, it must be pointed out that today's streets are far more dangerous than those of rural Missouri more than a hundred years ago, and the Mississippi River much less treacherous than the canyons of our city streets.

Another difference that distinguished teenage runaways during my tenure on the street from those of Mark Twain's era was the fact that there were almost as many girl runaways as there were boys. The runaways of the past who struck out for "The West" on a venture quest are also history. It is estimated that of recent runaways, seventy-five percent came from broken families and had suffered serious physical and/or sexual abuse.

For these wounded teenage street kids, the decision to run away from an emotionally and sometimes physically abusive home for the "glamour" of the streets sent them spiraling into what someone called, "a world of sweet-smelling Mercedeses and piss-stained alleys, of $75 tricks and $2 sandwiches." They lived in stinking hotel rooms. They went days without showering or sleeping. Their arms bled with abscesses from dirty needles. With their trust in adults blasted away, they lived numb and degraded lives; their spirits hardened, their hopes withered, their optimism faded, and their lives reduced to the next fix or the next sexual encounter. It was a painful life of deceit and denial.

Many homeless teenagers spent their limited savings in a matter of days after they reached the City (if they hadn't already been ripped-off). Defenseless and vulnerable, they had nowhere to go and no one to turn to. They ate at the several soup kitchens open to them. If they could afford a small room, a cheap meal, or had friends or family they could depend on for help, they might have been able to avoid a very tragic street life. Unfortunately, most couldn't and didn't. Most of the runaways and "pushaways" I knew came into the City with lofty dreams and high hopes of either escaping the restrictions of their home-life or making it big on their own. Many never made it out of the Bus Depot. They were met by smooth-talking con artists who offered them something to eat and a comfortable bed with "no strings attached." Before they knew what had happened, they were hooked on drugs and became a part of a pimp's harem. Thousands of these kids were buried in unmarked graves each year; they died alone, friendless and without their families knowing (sometimes not caring) about their deaths.

Most of the young people who came into San Francisco migrated to the Tenderloin or Polk Gulch areas. Why did so many of them come to these city blocks, notorious for their X-rated movie houses, massage parlors, and dingy hotels? They were in search of allies, anonymity and a better life. What they discovered was much different: a world of pimps, drug dealers, hunger, destitution, and, sometimes, death. Seen through the eyes of an idealistic young person, the action on the street could be frightening. Experiencing that action first-hand was even worse. Within weeks, many fell unwittingly into lives of prostitution and crime. Their lives lacked not only the guidance and attention all teenagers need, but also the regular meals, safe quarters, clean

San Francisco police detectives give advice on where to begin a search for a runaway girl.

clothes and showers most of us take for granted. Many of them thought that crack, prostitution, and violent pimps were the worst that street life could dish out to them. That was before AIDS!

I met Rick in early November, 1964. I was sitting in the Plush Doggie, an all-night, open-air diner, which used to be where the BART Station on Market and Powell now stands. I was visiting with Guy Straight, the Director of the Matachine Society. Rick walked in and immediately took over the conversation. He was a precocious exhibitionist, with a wise comeback for every remark. In spite of his braggadocio and apparent toughness, he spent the rest of the night with me. When we were alone, he began to lower his defenses and showed how frightened and desperate he really was.

Rick was a seventeen-year-old "pushaway" from Minnesota. His parents were divorced and his mother's new husband didn't want the boy around. He bought him a second-hand car and told him to leave. Rick eventually reached San Francisco. Jobs for seventeen-year-olds were not too plentiful. Especially scarce are those that will pay all expenses. That particular night he was feeling depressed and alone. A month or two before, while at this same diner, a man started a conversation with him and eventually offered to take him home. He offered Rick a few dollars for his "company" and the trap snapped. Rick then became a boy hustler, hanging out at the diner until someone picked him up. Since he was a clean-cut, baby-faced kid, someone always did. He hated what he was doing and loathed himself for doing it. He searched me out and spent as much time with me as his "business" would afford. He told me that he sometimes had sex with girls his own age but that despite finding it enjoyable, "it didn't earn me a buck!"

One night he invited me to his little one-bedroom apartment that he shared with another hustler. I found it strange that he slipped on a pair of tight-fitting leather gloves shortly after we got there. Gradually, this baby-faced kid began to reveal a part of his personality I hadn't seen before. In fact, it was an aspect I had not even suspected. Whenever we were together he was respectful, sensitive and often tender. This evening he shared with me his desire for and preoccupation with violence. Certain things fell into place. At our first meeting he wore a bandage on his throat, which he said came from a fight he had in the Tenderloin. On earlier visits he took me to the Chuckers and the Caboose, both very tough, gay leather bars where he sometimes went to pick up tricks. On that night, in his room, he showed me a six-inch switchblade and demonstrated how to use it to do the greatest damage. He also showed me a vicious-looking version of a small hay hook which can "rip out a man's guts with one swipe." He then told me how he could cut up a man's face by hitting him with tight-fitting leather gloves just like the ones he was wearing. Since he hated hustling, I suspect that he sometimes beat up his customers in order to prove his manliness.

When it came time for me to leave, he said he had been testing me. Because I had been good to him, he thought I might have a hidden agenda. He said he wasn't sure whether I was straight or gay and that if I had made a pass at him, he would have "beat the shit out of me!"

Rick's one great love was his automobile, which was being held in a shop in Oakland for repair bills. His goal in life was to earn enough to get it out of hock and head back to Minnesota. Soon after we met, I became his "banker." He knew that he didn't have enough discipline to save money on his own. So after turning a trick he would seek me out and give me a portion of his earnings to hold until he could get enough together.

One night he came and asked to withdraw his savings. He had enough to pay the repair and storage bill on his car. He left the next day and I never saw him again. Even a not-too-ideal home life was better than the streets! I heard from him once after he reached home, but not again. San Francisco was a bad dream better shoved way back in his collection of memories.

Tom was an innocent-looking sixteen-year-old from Florida who was running away from home because his parents "are too strict." They caught him kissing his girlfriend in his bedroom and put him on restriction for a week. He raided his savings box and scrounged enough money to buy a bus ticket to San Francisco, "where people can live as they please."

Within minutes of his getting off the bus I had to step in to rescue him. He was wearing an expensive leather jacket, and six or eight burley Hell's Angels riders decided it would look better on one of their "old ladies." They were pulling the jacket off this screaming, crying, frightened boy when I stepped into the fray, and yanked them off. Just as one of these giants (whose arms were bigger around than my waist) was about to knock me into the next county, another yelled, "Hey, he's a Father. Leave him alone." They then took off and the street was cleared of everyone except one frightened Night Minister and a scared and shivering young man. I found him a place to stay for the night and had him call his parents. A very relieved father flew out the next day to pick up his prodigal son. I doubt that Tom ever thought of running away again. He was one of the lucky ones.

Frank was not so fortunate. He was a nineteen-year-old from the Midwest, gullible and not too bright. About 3:00 a.m. I stopped at the YMCA hotel. Frank was waiting for me in the lobby, frightened out of his wits. He had unwittingly been involved in the robbery of a cigar store.

He went into the store with his friend Chuck not knowing (he said) that Chuck intended to commit a robbery. Since Chuck had held up the same store three times before, the clerk was ready for him when he walked in. Chuck pulled a gun, but the proprietor was faster and Chuck was shot. Frank and Chuck were able to reach their car and get away from the scene, but Chuck seemed in bad shape and passed out in the back seat. Frank panicked, abandoned both the car and his friend, and came to see me. I eventually found the car (Frank couldn't remember where he had parked it), crawled into the back seat and discovered that Chuck was dead.

Then followed the mechanics of the squad cars, the police lab, and eventually the questioning by homicide detectives. I stood in the chill of the morning for several hours with the body of a nineteen-year-old boy a few feet away, his lifeless face distorted by pain and fear. A thousand thoughts went through my mind as I stood there shivering, not so much from the cold without as from the emotions within. The street was dark and isolated and I thought of the fear this young man must have experienced as he felt his life slip away on the lonely back seat of an abandoned automobile.

I wondered about his background and what led him to this kind of a death. I wondered whether he would be missed and if there was anyone who cared how he died. I thought of my own son about the same age, in a warm bed in a home where he knows he is loved. Did someone love this young man, or was he like so many others I had met, unloved, uncared for and forgotten?

I looked at the dried blood on his face and chest. I stared at the pool of dry, black blood on the floor of the car, and Joan Baez's "Song in the Blood" kept going through my mind:

> Where's it going, all this spilled blood?
> blood of the blackjacked, of the humiliated,
> of suicides, of firing squad victims, of the condemned,
> and the blood of those that die just like that...
> In the streets a living being goes by with all his blood inside,
> suddenly there he is dead, and all his blood outside...

I shivered and went home. I wept in the arms of my wife and knew from my own experience how "Every man's death diminishes me."

It was a few days before Christmas. The billboards and magazine ads showed happy families gathered around the fireplace, smiling, warm and loving. They looked good, but how far from the truth they seemed! I again was in the bus depot. My beeper alerted me to a call from a twenty-year-old sailor just back in the States after a six-month tour of duty on a carrier. He was staying at the Shaw Hotel, only a block from the depot. I went up to his room and found a lonely and frightened young man. He had been drinking some, but was not drunk. He said he was afraid of becoming an alcoholic. Then suddenly he blurted out his real concern. He was on his way back to the Midwest for Christmas. When he called his parents to tell them that he was coming, he decided that it would be easier to tell them on the phone that he was gay than it would be in person. His father, a conservative Christian minister, was furious and rejected him completely. He told him he was no longer welcome in his home and that he was not to come for Christmas unless "he confesses his sins and changes his lifestyle." The young man sat on the couch, his head on his knees, uncontrollably sobbing out his fears, his hurt, his loneliness and his feeling of total worthlessness and rejection.

I reached out to lay my hand on his head but suddenly withdrew, afraid the touch might be misunderstood. And I was angry! Angry with myself for being afraid to express the only thing I had to offer at the moment, love for a boy who felt unloved. I was angry at a Puritanical society, that restricts so simple and Biblical an act as the touch of a hand to add life to otherwise dead words. I remembered how often Jesus laid his hands on those who came to him, "and they were healed." I reached out once more and laid my arm across his shoulders and the sobbing stopped.

It was difficult to work with this young man over the next week to help him realize that he was not as worthless as his father said he was and that he was still a child of God, no matter what his father's theology taught! It was difficult to make him believe that God had not deserted him, even though his parents had.

Proclaiming pious platitudes from the pulpit is not enough. Someone must respond to the desperate and painful cry in the middle of the night. This young sailor, as well as Tom and Frank and Bill and Susan and all the other kids on the street, must hear that someone cares and that God cares and is still concerned about them.

It was tough to talk about the traditional values of the Church to young people who didn't know what you were talking about. My values were often questioned, my theology challenged, my own motivation under suspicion.

It was easy for me to be judgmental of prostitutes and pimps and drug addicts and hustlers when I served a nice middle-class church where everyone lived normal, respectable and acceptably moral lives. It was easy to criticize "THEM" when I never had to look "THEM" in the eyes or hear first-hand the tragedy of their lives.

It was difficult to talk about being created in the image of God when you walk the worst streets in the City night after night. But this I know: whenever I encountered low views of what it means to be human, whenever I encountered those who had no regard for human life or human dignity, I also found a total disregard for the concept that the Spirit of God had been breathed into us, forging us into being truly human and truly brothers and sisters, one of the other.

I do not want to imply that all the kids on the street were pushaways. In fact, the vast majority were not. Many came from loving families that had no more difficulty than any family raising teenagers in a turbulent age. Not all parents were glad to see their rebellious children leave home. They often tried all means possible to dissuade them, but the abundance of stories about the Haight Ashbury with its promise of free drugs and free sex was more temptation than their children could resist, especially when their hormones were running wild.

Jared's well-to-do parents lived in the South Bay and provided him with everything they thought he wanted. They gave him a new car when he graduated from high school. They built a cottage on the property to give him privacy. When Jared told them he was gay they were disappointed; after all, he was their only son. But they didn't give up on him or disown him. They took him to a counselor, not to change him but in the hope that his gayness could possibly be a stage he would eventually outgrow. They gave me a picture of Jared. It was of a handsome young man who would stand out in any crowd.

They hadn't heard from him for six months and were concerned. They had gone to the police but got no help or encouragement from them. "The City is inundated with thousands of kids from all over the country," they were told. "Finding one in the crowd is almost an impossibility." They hired a well-known private detective who gave up after a month or two. As a last resort, they called me.

I felt I had a better chance of finding him than anyone else. I showed his picture around in the most promising spots. But my hustler acquaintances were hesitant to betray a friend until I ran into David, my friend from Pearls. "Oh, sure I know Jared; I've even scored with him. You can usually find him hustling on Market and Mason streets on Saturday night." That next Saturday, I began my rounds by cruising the young men on the street. As I suspected, Jared did stand out in the crowd. He was hesitant and suspicious at first. When I revealed some intimacies his parents had shared with me, he softened and questioned me about them. When I told him how much his mother missed him, he came close to tears.

Jared agreed to meet with them on the condition that I would also be present. I called his parents and set up a meeting for the next night at the United Church of Christ church on Post and Mason streets. The meeting was emotional, friendly and without rancor. Jared went home with his parents that night. They had some minor differences, but eventually settled down to a normal family lifestyle. They kept in touch for about a year. Then the calls became less and less frequent. It was obvious that they wanted that period in their lives closed. I was just a reminder of a time they wanted to forget.

Pat's parents came from a small desert town in Nevada. Hearing that I often stopped in at the YMCA several times during the night, they took their chances and waited in the lobby until I showed up. All they wanted, they said, "was for their daughter to be returned safely." Pat was fourteen and had run away with her seventeen-year-old boyfriend. They said he had no money. The parents suspected that the boy had turned Pat out on the streets to earn enough for them to eat and pay the rent.

The picture they showed me was of an attractive blond girl with an infectious smile. She looked familiar but I didn't want to raise their hopes by saying so. I got nowhere showing the picture around to my street people friends. Then, when I thought I had reached the end of my rope, I remembered Bonny Brae. I found Bonny at Chuckers. She was high but still alert enough to say, "Sure, I know her. She's been working the streets for several weeks. She lives in a hotel on Taylor Street just north of Turk."

The hotel was a flea-trap like so many others in the Tenderloin. The night clerk gave me no information until I suggested that I would tell the police he was renting rooms to minors. Suddenly, he became very cooperative and even offered to take me upstairs. I rode up to the room on a rickety, ancient, cage elevator, wondering whether it could possibly reach the fifth floor. The halls were dark and the carpets worn and smelly. The room was typical—dingy, with a filthy, broken-down, double bed pushed against the wall and a washbasin in the corner, which every man who rented the room used for a urinal.

The boy was surly and a smart aleck. Whenever I asked Pat a question he answered for her until I put a stop to it.

The boyfriend, Bob, was both verbally and physically abusive. It was obvious that she was afraid of him. Pat jumped at the chance to go back home. I arranged for a meeting between Pat and her parents for the next night at the YMCA. Bob said he would not be there. He refused to meet with those "fucking hypocrites" and proclaimed, "If you go back to your folks, that's the last you'll see of me." Pat seemed relieved.

The next evening was a real celebration. Pat went home with her parents. That was the last I saw or heard from them. I saw Bob hustling in Chuckers, but he was so filthy and unattractive that I doubt he scored very often. I tried to talk to him on several occasions but he always mumbled and walked away. He was usually high on something. Eventually, he disappeared from the streets. Bonny Brae told me that he had been arrested for beating up a john.

It was not always the goal of the Night Ministry to send runaways back into the environment from which they tried to escape. Sometimes the families were so dysfunctional that returning these young people was tantamount to child abuse. We made every effort to encourage the parents to seek counseling with a children's agency in their area. If that was not possible we suggested that the parents allow their child to stay in San Francisco at Huckleberry House, an excellent facility located in the heart of the Haight Ashbury. It provided counseling not only for the runaway but, if possible, for the parents as well.

When the Night Ministry was unable to locate a runaway, we recommended that the parents contact the Haight Ashbury Switchboard, a clearinghouse and liaison between parents and kids. It was a confidential message center where runaways could leave messages without fear of their location being revealed. They were required to call their parents simply to let them know that they were alive and well.

Another invaluable resource was the Haight Asbury Free Clinic started by a young doctor by the name of David E. Smith. The clinic provided free medical care, and counseling for young people surviving on the streets. Most had an inadequate diet and were sleeping out in all kinds of weather (San Francisco gets very cold at night). These kids contracted every communicable disease making the rounds: the ever-present pneumonia, hepatitis, ulcers from using dirty needles, and the sexually transmitted diseases which accompanied their promiscuity.

They were scared. They were lonely. They were isolated. They would like to go home again. But how does a seventeen-year-old "man" tell his mother he misses her?

I was unable to identify an end to the Hippy Era. It faded rather than ended. There are still wanna-be hippies in the Haight and even a few hard liners unable to let go of a lifestyle that in many ways was more fancy than fact.

CHAPTER 9

The Plight of the "Working Girl" or Boy

The weather in San Francisco is usually cold but during the rainy season, it is really cold! The rain is often in the form of San Francisco "fog," that indescribable mist that hangs in the air and permeates everything it touches. Sometimes it comes down in pounding sheets driven by howling winds, making it impossible to escape a bone-chilling soaking.

The prostitutes clustered in small groups in dark doorways talking about the expensive trick they turned last night, or last week. They found little warmth in each other's company, shivering in miniskirts that don't even show beneath their coats, their bony knees knocking in the cold. The male hustlers in tight jeans and short jackets or T-shirts were afraid to overdress lest they hide their wares. They leaned against the dripping buildings or, if they were desperate, stood at the curb ready to jump at the first offer that stopped.

Sometimes the prostitutes were thick on the streets. A dozen or more to the block would vie competitively for every male walking down the street. Sometimes even I was propositioned. When I was recognized, there followed an embarrassed, feeble attempt to apologize.

Once on Geary Street, her hair bleached an unbelievable blond color, like Kansas wheat in the middle of August, a "working girl" called to me but then found it difficult to speak. She was obviously troubled. Her eyes filled with tears. I knew how much courage it took to stop me, a clergyman, because whether I liked it or not, I was the symbol of judgment. I tried to make it easier for her. I took her hand and led her to phone booths, away from the ridiculing eyes

"Working Girls" hanging out together for protection and company.

of her "sisters." We talked, I in one and she in another, as though we were in a confessional. Tears streamed down her face as she told of her self-disgust and of her fear of a nervous breakdown. I encouraged her to seek out some long-term help and gave her several referrals that would cost her little or no money. I hoped that she would follow through in the morning. I gave her my card and told her to call me before she grew too desperate.

Encounters like this troubled me! No names exchanged, no call, no follow-up. Each night I walked the streets searching faces in the hope that I would see her again. Did she follow my advice? Did she seek professional help, which was available during the day? Did she swallow her pride and forget her promise to "make it on her own" and go back home? Or was she one of the many about whom I read on the back page of the morning paper—"An empty bottle of sleeping pills was found on her night stand."

Success stories in working with prostitutes were few and far between, for two rather significant reasons. The primary force that held them in the grip of their profession was the power their pimp wielded over them, by physical abuse as well as through psychological intimidation. Pimps kept their harems under control by beating them if they weren't aggressive enough or if they

The "Meat Rack" at Mason and Market Streets where boys hang out waiting for a John to pick them up, hopefully for more than one night.

held back on earnings. Sometimes prostitutes suffered this abuse if they took the initiative to talk to me. The beatings were always "discreet" so that no bruises were visible. The pimps also intimidated the girls to the degree that they felt worthless and completely incapable of making a life of their own.

The reason for my limited success working with prostitutes was their addiction to drugs, which were supplied by the pimps. If the girls (boys did not have pimps) didn't toe the line or turn enough tricks, a pimp would withhold drugs. This soon brought the girl around to doing what he wanted.

One creative and successful relationship developed with a prostitute. I met her on my way into a dingy and disreputable after-hours club on Mason Street. After-hours clubs were supposedly coffee houses that opened at 2:00 a.m. when the bars closed. They were licensed to serve snacks, coffee and soft drinks, but usually also sold liquor served in coffee cups. It was amazing how many cups fell to the floor whenever a policeman walked through the door!

Coffee Don's was down a long flight of stairs, which led to a dimly lighted room, sparsely furnished and filled with ear-blasting music from a decrepit juke box. It was a miserable, rainy night, and I was willing to go anywhere to get away from the weather. Halfway down the stairs I met a rather voluptuous woman on the arm of an obvious tourist. When she saw me, she stopped short and asked where I was going. When I told her I was going for a cup of coffee, she said, "Not without me, Father!" She took me by the arm and started to lead me down the stairs. After an astonished moment, her john blurted out, "Hey, what about my money?" Mildred reached down into her cleavage, pulled out some bills and handed them to him, leaving him standing with mouth agape, wondering what charms I had that he didn't.

That first meeting resulted in a counseling relationship that lasted almost a year. Mildred was left a widow at an early stage in her marriage, without skills and with a child to rear. She had danced a little when she was a girl, although not professionally. She was pretty, well built, had all the skills and equipment necessary to be a topless dancer, but that work didn't earn her enough to support her daughter who was ready for college. She would meet some patrons after her club closed to supplement her income. Her daughter knew nothing of her after-hours prostitution, and Mildred was terrified that she would find out. She despised herself for what she did but felt trapped. She was a fallen-away Roman Catholic and wanted to get back into the Church, but didn't feel worthy. She was certain no priest would understand her lifestyle or would even try to help.

A member of my Night Ministry Board was the co-owner of an agency that supplied temporary office and secretarial help for companies throughout the City. He offered to take her on and pay for her training to develop some skills that could bring her an income that could support her and her daughter. I introduced her to a Franciscan priest I knew who was assigned to St. Boniface Church on Golden Gate Avenue. That church was committed to working with the disenfranchised in the downtown area of San Francisco. The priest was understanding and sympathetic. He helped her to return to the Church and to again receive the Sacrament she so missed. She eventually decided to move back to Washington where she could get away from the influences of the City and be close to her mother. She returned to the mainstream of life and her daughter never discovered her secret.

Other relationships were more transient and less satisfying. An eighteen-year-old male hustler wearing a light jacket and black, skin-tight pants (both soaked) stopped me. He was coughing and obviously ill. "I haven't turned a trick in over a week. I don't have a place to stay. I haven't eaten in two days." I got him a meal and a room for the night. I met with him a few more nights and then he disappeared. Contacts like this would make me wonder how effective a Night Pastor I was. Had I, in some small way at least, been able to convey to him the love of God and the concern of the Church? Did he know that I prayed for him? Would he remember that once on a miserable cold night when he was down on his luck, the Church was there, and cared?

Although the majority of the "working" girls and boys were from broken or dysfunctional homes, they still longed for a family life of some kind. Most of the young hustlers clustered together in small groups on street corners or doorways, joking, pushing, wrestling, sharing a joint, and acting like teenagers on a thousand other street corners in a thousand other cities and towns. They did anything that would make them feel a part of the group, anything that would take away some of the loneliness and fear so prevalent among those living on the streets.

Eventually, they would break off into small groups of several couples. They would rent a room in a cheap hotel and live communally. One night it would be the responsibility of one to earn enough money for rent and food, the next that of one of the others. In this way each got a reprieve from the streets for a couple of nights. They became very protective of one another and loved and supported each other, as few blood family members were willing to do.

It was not unusual for me to come across couples of individuals both of whom worked the streets earning their living through prostitution. One young couple, not yet out of their teens, from a small ranching town in Idaho were married in a traditional wedding back home. They immediately took off for California to make it big in the music industry. It didn't work out that way.

Soon she was pregnant. He had no marketable skills, so he turned to hustling. By the time their baby was a year old, their situation hadn't improved so she entered the trade. They would take turns caring for their baby while the other worked the streets. Often, after they both had meaningless sex with pretended affection and feigned orgasms, they would go back to their room for their private, loving, sexual relationship.

The older, more experienced prostitutes who worked the streets were as competitive as any upwardly mobile young women in any other profession. Like cats, they might circle each other, hiss and scratch and pretend hostility. But let one of them experience trouble and the others responded to the cry for help immediately. Once I saw a john who had tried to stiff a prostitute. He shoved her out of the cab without paying her and yelled for the driver to drive away. The driver refused, and the trick was left defenseless on the street, surrounded by eight or ten prostitutes swinging their spike-heeled shoes. His face was in shreds before the police came to his rescue. No arrests were made and the night drifted back into some sense of normalcy.

This event gave me a sense of security. I knew that these "immoral street walkers" would rush to my aid if I needed them.

CHAPTER 10

San Francisco High

Almost every jukebox bellowed out the location of Tony Bennett's heart. The cable cars clanged their warning to wary and hesitant out-of-state drivers terrified at facing the intimidating hills. Nightclub barkers bellowed, "Bigger and better boobs inside!" The ladies of the night invited all and sundry up "for a little fun you can't find down on the farm." And yet I loved this City as I have never loved any other place in my life. It was my life!

Summer always saw an invasion of the hordes. Herb Caen's "Baghdad-by-the-Bay" brought people from all over the world. There was the tourist from the Midwest, the conventioneer from the East, even native a Californian escaping the heat of the Valley. Europeans and Asians were not immune. They came from all the corners of the world. Crowds blocked the traffic at Powell and Market, pushing and shoving to get on the next cable car. The incomparable cars, like the engine in *The Little Engine That Could*, grunted and groaned and strained under a three times capacity load as they began the almost insurmountable climb to the top of Nob Hill.

Along with the tourists came the young starry-eyed neo-Hippies looking for a Utopia. This "Utopia" existed only in their minds and in the writings of music and verse written by self-proclaimed idealists, many of whom had, somewhere along the line, lost touch with reality.

These young people came with the expectation of being cared for by some great nebulous "family" that would feed and house them. If no agency or responsible person interceded within the first few days of their arrival, they would be introduced to drugs and the downward spiral would begin. Drugs were supplied freely by pushers. They knew that once these young people were hooked, they would be regular customers. Their "free gifts" would be paid for many-fold. The youngsters' bright starry eyes soon turned to dull and expressionless "starey" eyes. The luster of their lives became as tarnished as the luster of the City.

I was snapped out of my semi-trance one evening by the sound of my pager. It was a call from Suicide Prevention. "A young girl needs help," said the volunteer, "but we don't know where she is. Can you hang on while we trace the call?" Anxious, nervous, moments passed until the tracer came through and I had an address to go on. I found a pretty, nineteen-year-old girl literally cringing on the floor in the corner of her seventh floor studio apartment. She was afraid to go near the window where a fountain in the courtyard below was reaching out its arms, calling her to jump. She said she had taken a smorgasbord of drugs during the previous twelve hours. These left her in a totally confused state of mind. I doubted that she actually ingested the variety of drugs she rattled off, but there was no doubt in my mind that she was high.

By the time I reached her she was hysterical. Though she argued with me about my "smug faith," I was at least able to keep her mind off her fears and the call of the fountain. Several hours later, she came "down" from her trip and relaxed enough for me to leave. Before I left, I was able to persuade her to allow me to call her boyfriend (literally the "boy next door" from her hometown in the Midwest).

He came over immediately and reluctantly agreed to stay with her for a few days until she either came down completely or checked herself into a treatment center. He was a very straight, nice looking young man who was growing weary of her drug use. However, he cared enough about her to be willing to give the relationship another chance. I called several times within the next few weeks, but she refused to talk to me. About a year later, she called to apologize for that bad period in her life and to tell me that she was now "clean and sober" through the help of Alcoholics Anonymous and was at last getting her life together.

The Tenderloin has always been associated with crime and I saw my share of it. Sometimes the crime was violent. Sometimes it wasn't for nickels and dimes, but for larger stakes. Violent street crime usually involved drugs and often included death. One night while walking past a dingy hotel on Mason Street noted for its drug pushing, a young man stumbled into my arms from a darkened doorway. I grabbed him, thinking he was drunk, but as I eased him to the sidewalk I felt a sticky, warm dampness ooze between my fingers. He had been stabbed in the back.

Even though I had witnessed a great deal of violence in my years on the streets and had seen a substantial amount of bloodshed, I still had to fight back panic as I held that young man in my arms. I helplessly watched his life's fluid end up as a dark patch on a dirty, garbage-strewn sidewalk. After the police and ambulance took him away, I went to the YMCA and washed my hands. But though the dry blood easily washed away, the glassy stare, the look of horror on this boy's face as he realized that he had only moments to live, can never be washed from my memory! I shivered, though it wasn't cold. Later, a policeman called from Mission Emergency Hospital to tell me "John Doe was DOA." It was the Christmas season, but "Peace on earth, good will toward men" seemed so far from real.

Not all calls came from the Tenderloin or less affluent districts of the City. Some came from Pacific Heights, Nob Hill or from the more up-scale hotels. A call came one night from Cecil, a forty-four-year-old man staying at the Fairmont Hotel, who was contemplating suicide. He was born and raised in London and after finishing his schooling, began work at a British bank with a branch in Hong Kong. He lived there for more than twenty years. Some time during his early years there, Cecil became addicted to heroin. He said it was inexpensive and easy to buy on the street. He was able to pack enough into his luggage when he went back to England for a visit to his family, but not enough to last indefinitely. He had turned down several offers for advancement from his home office. This time he faced not an offer but an ultimatum: either accept the advancement and return to the home office in London or be made "redundant." Cecil was terrified by the prospect of moving back to London where he believed he would suffer severe punishment if his addiction were discovered.

Fortunately I was able to convince him that the attitude in Great Britain toward addiction was much more enlightened than that in the United States. I assured him that the approach was more toward rehabilitation than punishment. The government had clinics where withdrawal was handled through a gradual process of reduced administration of drugs plus counseling. I told him of Life Line, an agency in London similar to the Night Ministry, and was able to give him the name of a doctor I had housed and fed when he was stranded in San Francisco as a young student. About a year later I received a note from Cecil thanking me and simply saying, "All is well."

In the early days of the Night Ministry, I rode with the S-Squad (Saturation Squad), a special unit of the police force that saturated an area with unmarked cars when an emergency arose. I eventually stopped the practice because riding with the police gave me a bad reputation with my street friends.

One night, while riding with the S-Squad, we were called to a flophouse on the Embarcadero to assist in a drug bust. After the bust came down, the officers made a "social call" on an old prostitute friend living in the same building. She was way past her prime, had just shot-up and was nodding. She had blotches of infections up and down her arms from using dirty needles, and was selling her "charms" in more filth and squalor than I had ever seen. Yet, hanging over her bed was a three-foot Picasso print! This gave me a hint of the kind of person she had been. I couldn't help but wonder, along with poet Edwin Markham (in his poem "The Man With the Hoe") "Whose breath blew out the light within this brain?"—and remember another woman in the same profession in the ancient past. I heard all too faintly the words, "Let him who has not sinned cast the first stone." I could find no stone to throw.

Sometimes the momentum built from years of destructive behavior was impossible to check. I had just arrived home one Sunday morning when the clerk at the YMCA called. A young man I had counseled through a referral from Suicide Prevention had slashed his wrists and would talk to no one but me. I rushed back downtown, persuaded him to go with me to Mission Emergency Hospital only to have an insensitive and unsympathetic doctor antagonize him to the point of causing him to leave.

I cleaned him up and bandaged him as best I could, and the next night persuaded him to go back to the hospital. The reception on Monday night was just the opposite of what it had been the night before. With a caring young doctor's help, I was able to persuade him to check into the North East Community Mental Health Center where he spent several weeks.

I saw him every night and believed he was making progress. Then he disappeared. I ran into him on the street a week after his disappearance and found him back into the same old routine of drugs and hustling to support his habit. He was heading in the same direction as on the night when he first called, a dead end route! The Beatles could have written their song, "Nowhere Man," about him:

He's a real nowhere man
Sitting in his nowhere land
Making all his nowhere plans for nobody.

It was raining. Usually I disliked the rain, but tonight it was refreshing. The streets were dirty, the sidewalks littered. Often the City had a tired, used look. The gentle rain bathed the streets and refreshed the air, giving the City and inhabitants alike the hope for a good, clean start. I stood on Market Street, alone and cold. The misty rain formed eerie halos around the streetlights. I watched a trickle of water run down the side of a building and slither along the sidewalk like some magic, ever-growing, silver serpent.

The theatergoers had long since gone home. The tourists shivered in their hotel rooms. The hustlers straggled back to wherever hustlers straggle. I thought no one was on the streets so I was startled when someone slipped into the doorway next to me and said, "Hi, Don!" Mark was an old friend whom I could no longer help. Ordinarily he was neat and good-looking, but not tonight. He was desperate for a fix. "I need twenty bucks, Don. I'll do anything you want, you name it. Anything! What kind of sex do you like? Fifteen bucks? Ten?" How desperately I wanted to help, but there wasn't a thing I could do for him. My eyes misted over and welled up with tears, or maybe it was just the rain.

Mark was someone I really cared about. I saw him regularly and often visited with him in his room. I had an opportunity to get to know him in some depth. He was exceptionally good looking with a bright smile and a great sense of humor. Although his formal education was limited, he was well read and intelligent. He had an "old lady" with whom he lived and with whom he fathered two beautiful sons. He seemed to have everything going for him except one—drugs! He and his girlfriend each shot-up several hundred dollars worth of heroin a day, an amount neither could earn legitimately. Both prostituted themselves and Mark often robbed or blackmailed his customers to satisfy his addiction.

I believed in Mark so much and trusted him so completely that once I covered a thousand dollar bail bond on a burglary charge, only to have him disappear! This was money I didn't have! I visited the judge in his chambers and, although the judge was understanding, he gave me only twenty-four hours to find him. I contacted a policeman friend who was off duty and we went on an all night search of Mark's old haunts. Just as dawn was breaking, I found him holed-up in a miserable flophouse. I didn't let him out of my sight until I was able to get him to court at 9:00 a.m. that morning. It so happened that the prosecuting attorney was also a friend of mine. He persuaded his client to agree to a plea bargain and Mark was given probation rather than prison.

I did as much as I was capable of doing to help Mark and the mother of his children work for change in their lives, but to no avail. Eventually, I had to perform the most difficult task in my entire Night Ministry years: my daughter Kathy and I went to his apartment, and while he was in a drug stupor, we took his children to Juvenile Hall and arranged that they be removed from his care. Mark was devastated; his "old lady" didn't care. Mark loved his sons, but he loved heroin more! He was angry for what had happened, but not with me. He was angry with himself for being so stupid as to allow himself to get into a situation that resulted in the loss of his children. In the long run he knew that what I did showed more love for his children than he did when drugs were in control of his life.

The loss of his sons woke Mark up to the realization that his life was going nowhere and that drugs were robbing him of that which he loved the most. He signed himself into an intensive residential treatment facility and after two years established himself in a job in a city away from San Francisco. I eventually was able to help him regain custody of his boys.

The busiest season of the year was always between Thanksgiving and New Year's, but this December 22nd was an unusually quiet one. It was warm and spring-like. I had stopped in a little cafe on the corner of Ellis and Leavenworth when I got a call from the dispatcher at the Greyhound bus depot. He had a distraught woman in his office who needed my help. I found a petite, elderly woman who was almost hysterical until she saw my collar, which comforted her enough to make it possible for us to communicate.

Twenty-five years earlier she had lost her husband who left few resources to support her and her infant son, John. She went to work for a cleaning service in Seattle and was able to earn enough to help John get through college and also earn a graduate degree in chemistry the preceding June. He found a job in the Bay Area and had recently moved to the City. He and his mother had looked forward to spending Christmas together.

She got off the bus the evening of the 22nd carrying two shopping bags. One contained a few items of clothing and some toiletries, and the other had

Christmas gifts for John. But John wasn't at the bus depot to meet her. She had talked to him the night before, and was certain there had been no misunderstanding about her arrival time. She called his apartment, but got no answer. When he didn't show up, she continued to call, without success. She didn't know anyone else to call. She suspected that an emergency had come up at work or that he might have been caught in traffic.

She picked up a newspaper to occupy her mind while she was waiting and there read the news of John's death. He and a woman co-worker were driving into the City from work when someone driving at a high rate of speed entered the freeway from an off ramp and hit their car head on, killing all three. The driver of the offending car was under the influence of drugs and alcohol.

The shock for John's mother was tremendous. She knew no one in San Francisco. She had no place to go since she had intended to stay with her son. As we continued to talk she calmed down and we were able to make plans for her housing and for the shipping of her son's body back to Portland. I called a funeral home, which had been helpful to me in the past. When I explained the circumstances of the situation, they agreed to take care of all arrangements at no charge.

John's mother asked if I was an Episcopal priest. When I told her I was not, she almost apologetically said she would like to receive the Sacrament, but from an Episcopal priest. By this time it was almost three in the morning. Bob Cromey, an Episcopal priest on the Night Ministry Board was someone I knew I could call without concern for the time. He came immediately and held a dignified, though unusual, communion service in the dispatcher's office. The altar was the cluttered dispatcher's desk. The "Eternal Light" came from a single light fixture with a green glass shade hanging from the ceiling and the only bells were from the phone. But the Words were ancient and holy and more meaningful than I had ever experienced.

I made a call to the manager of John's apartment house and explained our predicament. He had not heard about John's accident and said he would "act dumb" if the police came to seal off the apartment for any reason. I drove John's mother to the apartment and helped her get settled. She asked me to help her find John's address book. While she was looking for it in the bedroom, I searched the desk. In a bottom drawer, I found a stash of marijuana. I saw no reason to show it to his mother so I excused myself to go to the bathroom where I flushed it down the toilet. I left her alone that night. She said that was the way she wanted it to be. Bob arranged to have some women from his parish come in the next day to get John's personal things together to ship back to Portland. That was the last I saw or heard from her.

Sometimes the success of a night didn't depend on the quantity of calls, but on their quality. On one slow night when the calls were rather routine, a young man phoned at 4:30 a.m. He had seen one of our ads, and called to ask what the Night Ministry was all about. I began an explanation although I suspected that the reason for his call was deeper and more personal than that. We talked for an hour and a half during which time he told me about his drug habit, job problems as a result of drugs, and the alienation from his family. We talked, and I counseled, probed and even gently prodded. I promised to see him at the end of the week.

When I visited, he was really on a high, but this time it wasn't from drugs. He had followed my advice and called his mother after four years of no contact! She was ecstatic. "This my son was dead, and is alive again." The relationship was restored and with a combination of his determination, his family's help and the support of a drug program offered through the company where he worked, he was still "clean and sober" two years later when he was transferred to an overseas position.

All drug counseling relationships did not have a happy ending. In fact, most ended unhappily. A twenty-year-old man had checked into the Turk Street YMCA after having dropped a cap or two of acid. He went to his room on the eighth floor, and when the drug started to take effect, his hallucinations were frightening enough for him to call the desk for help. The clerk called an ambulance and he was taken to San Francisco General Hospital. The young intern psychiatrist, with little experience in drug treatment, released him with, "All you need is a good night's sleep." He returned to the YMCA, picked up his key, went to the eighth floor and without even going to his room, dove through the hall window, landing on the roof of my car. He died instantly. I had been called by the desk clerk, but arrived too late.

The most life threatening experience I had in all my years on the street was drug related. A naive, homeless teenager I had befriended was ripped off by a pusher whom I knew by sight and miserable reputation. The boy asked me to help him get his money back. I went with him to a flophouse on Turk street between Mason and Taylor and walked into a room filled with thousands of dollars worth of drugs and drug paraphernalia. While I was arguing with the pusher, my beeper went off, and before I knew what was happening, I was grabbed from behind and a knife was held to my throat. The pusher accused me of being a "narc" (Federal drug agent) and of signaling my partners. This was a time before beepers were common and mine was the first he had ever seen. I said, "Yes, I am a narc and our conversation is being picked up on my two-way radio." I told him that I had backup downstairs, and if I didn't walk out of there unharmed, he was a dead man. Fortunately, I was convincing enough for him to believe me and I and my young friend walked out safely. We didn't get the boy's money back, but by then, neither of us cared. The pusher disappeared from the streets and I never saw him again. My street reputation was tarnished for only a brief time before the event was forgotten.

One of the side problems of working with my particular "parish" was that it was transient. People with whom I worked one week would be gone the next. Sometimes that was good, as in this instance, but there were times I was left with an empty hole inside me when someone I came to care about disappeared, never to be heard from again.

Sometimes humor was intermingled with pathos as in the call I received from a young man who said he was in the process of committing suicide. I went to his apartment, kicked in the door, and found him in the bathroom. He had taken a bottle of Nembutals and had drunk a fifth of wine. He was submerged in a tub of water, bubbles rising to the surface, naked, but still wearing his horn-rimed glasses! I pulled the plug in the tub and there we sat, he naked and shivering in the empty tub and I on the stool. We talked for four hours before I was satisfied that he wouldn't try again. From then on, whenever he felt depressed, he called just to talk. He knew he was no longer alone.

Shortly after I got to the office one night, Chuck Lewis, my partner, called to say that Tim, a young man he had met on the street and befriended, was high on something and was heading for the bridge to commit suicide. Chuck tried to trace his route from North Beach to the bridge and I headed for the bridge itself. Chuck had notified the police so we felt we had the approach covered. As I drove up to the bridge I saw Tim running to reach the rail. I jumped out of my car and raced after him but the police reached him first. While we were talking to the police, a young man rushed up to tell the police that someone's car had rolled across the parking lot and rammed his car from the rear, nearly shoving him and his girlfriend into the Bay! When I had jumped out of my car to run for Tim, I neglected to set my emergency brake and my mistake almost resulted in serious consequences.

CHAPTER 11

Crumbling Foundations

How long will you judge unjustly and show favour to the wicked?
You ought to give judgement for the weak and the orphan,
and see right done to the destitute and downtrodden,
you ought to rescue the weak and the poor,
and save them from the clutches of wicked men.
But you know nothing, you understand nothing, you walk in the dark
while earth's foundations are giving way.

—Psalm 82:2–5, New English Bible

Sometimes wounds were inflicted by those who were supposed to be the protectors. I saw Jimmy sitting on a fireplug on the corner of Mason and Market streets at 1:30 in the morning. He was a very nice looking boy with jet-black curly hair and a husky build. When I approached him, the three or four older hustlers talking to him hurriedly scattered. Jimmy was fourteen! He had arrived in San Francisco that afternoon with his mother, stepfather and younger brother. His stepfather had taken him to Market Street and told him that he was to stay there until some "nice man" picked him up who would pay him to "play some games." The boy had not eaten since breakfast. I took him to Sam's for a meal (which he ate ravenously) and then walked him back to the flophouse south of Market where he was staying. When we got to his room, Jimmy asked me to wait in the hall while he went in to get his stepfather. As soon as he opened the door, the man began hollering and swearing. When Jimmy returned, he said his parents were having sex and his stepfather didn't want to talk to me.

Jimmy and I walked down the hall, climbed out on the fire escape and talked for some time. He wasn't the only one his stepfather put on the street to hustle. On occasion he did the same with Jimmy's younger brother who was only ten. The boys hated what their stepfather made them do. Jimmy said he was sometimes hurt by the men who picked him up. We talked about alternatives. He jumped at the opportunity of getting away from his stepfather and even his mother, who he said used drugs. I called a juvenile officer friend of mine who immediately came to the hotel with the police. The mother and stepfather were arrested and the two children were removed from their custody. As the children were taken away, Jimmy ran to me, threw his arms around my neck, hugged me and whispered in my ear, "Thanks, Father." In spite of being exposed to a life most people never imagine possible, he was still an innocent and naive fourteen year old.

My responsibility as a Christian counselor in one of the worst sections of the City was to make possible the opportunity for the struggling young man or woman to make those choices that could lead to a fuller and more satisfying lifestyle. At times it was difficult for me not to be judgmental of a man or woman like these boys' parents. It was my job to help people, as far as possible, to live lives of wholeness. Perhaps I gave these boys that opportunity.

In 1967, during the Summer of Love, it was estimated that San Francisco and Los Angeles had about 1,500 children and young people between twelve and twenty on the streets every night. Some of these were children who had, in many instances, created their own hell. They had chosen to leave good homes with loving and understanding parents for a life of freedom, drugs, sex, and independence. The vast majority, though, found themselves on the streets because they had been sinned against by family members, by teachers, by clergy, by those they had trusted—all too often by so-called "respectable" members of society.

A wealthy San Francisco businessman was a candidate for public office. His advertisement pitches splashed on billboards and flashed across TV screens. This man was arrested and found guilty of plying teenage street girls with money, drugs, and alcohol in exchange for sex. Another San Franciscan, a well-known millionaire, pled no contest for the same crime against teenaged boys and girls.

A couple of nights a week, I met a Roman Catholic priest who was cruising on the corner of Turk, Mason and Market streets near the door of the Blackcrow Bar. He made no effort to hide his identity. He taught at one of the universities. On occasion, he had one of his students with him. He liked young hustlers (fourteen- or fifteen-year-olds) and they liked him because he was gentle and respectful and because he didn't like "kinky" sex. Also, he was generous with his payment. He had some favorites with whom he would meet regularly. A few of the boys, especially Catholic ones, felt he was a hypocrite for more than one reason.

A hotel owner kept a room open all the time to use when he picked up a boy. He was a contributor to charitable causes and often sponsored fundraisers for a variety of charities in the City. He never did so for the Night Ministry because he knew that we worked against what he was doing to our street kids. One of his demands was that his wife observe him having sex with the boys. The hustlers thought this disgusting.

These men were leaders in the community, so-called "respectable members of polite society"—men thought to be persons to look up to and emulate. If our children couldn't look up to them, who could they look up to? Who are the role models for today's youth?

That was one of the stock questions I asked street kids when I could get them mellowed out enough to have a serious conversation. The answers were often startling:

"My big brother; he's in a gang and beats up people every day. He works around 6th and Howard rolling drunks."

What about your parents? Are they a good influence? Do they set a good example for you? Are they good role models?

"Naw. My mother's drunk all day and my old man's in jail for pushing drugs."

Suffering from alcohol, drugs, and homelessness, and still in need of the touch of a friendly hand.

When these children left home, traveling to cities hundreds of miles away, with little or no money in their pockets, it wasn't necessarily out of rebellion; it may have been an act of survival.

The City cried and I felt her pain, although at times I felt helpless. I understood Jesus as he stood above his favorite city and wept, "O Jerusalem, Jerusalem, would that I could gather you as a mother hen gathers her chicks." When I took the hand of a young girl, shivering and scared because it's her first night working the streets alone, or held in my arms a teenage boy who was crying and fighting back nausea after having had his first experience as a male hustler, the words I seemed to hear were not "You promised me...", but "You fed me. You clothed me. You visited me."

It is easy to throw oneself into sweeping movements where the touch of the personal is often secondary to luxuriating in abstract, self-righteous anger. But anger is not what I felt looking into the eyes of a troubled youth across the table of a darkened coffee house, hearing him say, "Yeah, life on the street sucks, but it ain't as bad as living at home." And this same street-wise fifteen-year-old, who lost his innocence all too long ago, added, "If you don't reach out to me, how can I reach out to you?"

Somehow, somewhere, there must be answers to at least some of these questions. They can be found in a loving family, but if that family is dysfunctional, support must come from the community. The supportive family does not have to be traditional, but it does have to be loving! It is not a hollow cliché that, "It takes a whole community to raise a child."

Just as no individual remains static and unchanged over a period of years, neither do cities. History and simple demographics change their characters and personalities. I do not think it is an exaggeration to say that there is not a city in our country which is not wounded in some way and which is not crying out because of that wound. The author of the book of Lamentations wrote:

> How lonely sits the city that was full of people! How like a widow she has become, she that was great among the nations! She that was a princess among the cities has become a vassal. All her people groan as they search for bread: they trade their treasures for food to revive their strength. They cry to their mothers, "Where is bread and wine?" and faint like the wounded in the streets of the city, as their life is poured out on their mother's bosom.

Neglect, abuse, and age are hurting our cities and leaving them not only wounded, but bleeding to death—bleeding from a hemorrhage which cannot be stayed by a mere transfusion. A transfusion merely revitalizes that which already exists. We need more than a transfusion! We need more than revitalization!

What we need is renewal—our cities need to be reborn with a different spirit, with different goals that will lead us away from selfishness, isolation, loneliness, and stoic independence. We need to go back to a sense of community and concern not only for me and my family and maybe for the family next door, but also for the stranger on the other side of town.

I was raised within the protection of the institutional Church. Its walls gave me security, but it doesn't give security to everyone. Our world is forever changing. Our cities are changing. They are becoming more and more complex and progressively more impersonal. The traditional language of the Church is no longer understood. New forms and new modes of ministry must be found to speak to a generation that will perish without it.

The Night Ministry was not the Church nor was it a substitute for the Church. The gathered faith community is still the Church and is still a vital instrument for change in the world today. The Church must not be stagnant or even self-perpetuating. It must be completely unselfish and outpouring. It must be constantly alert to the age in which it lives and must constantly seek new ways to speak to a civilization that will continue to flounder without it.

The night is like a hungry, predatory hunter, and the disorder and darkness of the streets are only the symbols of the darkness and disorder that has taken over the lives of so many. Although we know that "the light shines in the darkness and the darkness shall not overcome it," somehow, somewhere, the darkness has overcome the lives of both old and young alike. For too many, the search for the Holy Child is a pure but meaningless myth. For too many, hope is a lost word in his or her vocabulary and the desire for a higher life no longer exists.

It is tough to talk about traditional spiritual and moral values to young people whose lives have never been touched by those values. It is tough to talk about being created in the image of God when you walk the worst streets in the City night after night. But this I know: whenever I encountered low views of what it means to be human, whenever I encountered those who had no

Another friendly hand.

regard for human life or human dignity, I also found a total disregard for the concept that the Spirit of God had been breathed into us—that is, making us truly human and truly brothers and sisters one of the other. But how do you communicate these views? Verbal communication is not enough. Preaching is the last thing a young person wants to hear when the bottom has just fallen out of his or her life.

Even though I worked intimately with people in the Tenderloin for almost seventeen years, I in no way considered myself an expert in solving the overwhelming difficulties facing our urban centers. I believe that it is impossible to point to New York or Chicago or any other major urban center and proclaim: "This is the answer to urban blight. This is the answer to racial conflict. This is the answer to gang activity." But I do believe that it is possible to point to San Francisco and say, "These are the problems of San Francisco, and these are the solutions appropriate for solving those problems."

How often I saw the foundations crumble beneath the lives of individuals who were helpless to either prevent or correct the destruction! I met innumerable people caught in a maze of circumstances beyond their control, or leading a life dictated by a long history of past behavior. To break the pattern, to create an atmosphere for a "conversion experience," a change of life, an adaptation to a different lifestyle, was often difficult and sometimes impossible.

The rain came down, softly at first, drop-by-drop, picking up momentum until the sky seemed to suddenly split wide open and all of heaven shed its tears on the world below. The rain stopped and the City smelled fresh and newly laundered. The night people crept back into the streets, but all they found was each other. The tricks and johns alike were warm in bed, but not with each other. There is a softness about the night. The quietness enveloped me and I almost felt serene. Suddenly a howl, anguished and painful, reverberated like a roll of thunder through the empty streets. I hurried over and found a drag queen sprawled out on the wet sidewalk. I assumed she had been injured or beaten. I touched her shoulder, but she pulled away and snarled for me to leave her alone. I asked if she was ok. "Yes!" I asked if I could help get her home. "No! Leave me alone!" I held her hand, and she buried her head on my arm and sobbed. She had picked up a young sailor who was disgusted with both himself and her. When he found out that "she" was really a "he," he beat her up. Although he physically hurt her, his words were more painful than the beating. I left her lying on a cold, wet, gray sidewalk the color of despair. As much as I wanted to help, Bonny Brae's injury was one I couldn't heal. This was the last time I saw this loving, caring person.

Sometimes I experienced real miracles. My beeper called me to an elderly Russian widow living in one room in the Portrero district. It was extremely difficult for her to communicate in English, but she eventually got across to me that her husband had served as one of the Czar's personal bodyguards. He was killed during the Revolution and she was able to escape into China where she was helped by Baptist missionaries to eventually get to the United

States. Because of their kindness, she became a Baptist, which only isolated her more from the few Russian acquaintances she had in San Francisco who were Russian Orthodox. She was poor, living on welfare. She missed her husband. She had no children and she was terribly lonely. She saw no reason to live and wanted to take her own life. But first she would like to talk to a Russian speaking Baptist minister! An impossible request, I thought, but promised to do what I could. The promise was only a delaying tactic to keep her alive for at least one more day.

The very next day I was aroused from my sleep by a call from Valley Forge where the headquarters for the American Baptist Church was located. The American Baptist Home Missionary Society was one of my supporting denominations and they were wanting some information in order to continue their funding. No one from that office had ever called before or since. After we discussed the information they were seeking, I asked what I thought was a ridiculous question: "Do you, by any chance, know of a Russian-speaking, Baptist minister living in the Bay Area?" Without hesitation he gave me the name of a person living in San Mateo, a few miles south of San Francisco. I called and found him very sympathetic. He went to the distraught Russian lady immediately. That is, without a doubt, the most dramatic and swift-acting miracle I have ever experienced!

The changing seasons of the year have an effect on people. Christmas comes in the midst of the darkest time of the year. Darkness comes early and stays late. Darkness settles low over the dingy city buildings and makes the dirty streets and cluttered doorways more depressing than usual. The rain pelts down and, for a moment, the air is fresh and the streets are washed. The rain stops, and as if some diabolic painter were at work, the streets and buildings are immediately returned to their same dingy disarray. The last quarter of the year is supposed to be the happy quarter, filled with family gatherings and anticipated reunions. Tables almost collapse beneath the weight of food only a small army could consume. The cheery sound of tinkling bells beside the Salvation Army kettles, the round and bearded Santas "Ho Ho Ho"-ing heartily at the simple requests of innocent-eyed children, the piped in Muzak telling us, "'Tis the season to be jolly." All remind us that this is holiday time when everybody is supposed to be filled with warmth and cheer, and aglow with happiness.

It was Thanksgiving Day and I was on duty. I had just left a house full of friends after finishing a meal as traditional as Whittier's poems. My heart was warm, my stomach full, and I was comfortable. Surely no one could have less than I! Everyone must have had as satisfying a Thanksgiving Day as I had. I was walking down Market Street almost oblivious to the people around me, thinking of family and others I loved. I was suddenly jolted back to reality by a gravelly voice saying, "Hey, Padre, can you spare some change? I really need a drink." I found myself staring blankly into the dirty face of an old man. Deep, almost scar-like wrinkles covered his face. The stubble of gray beard gave him the appearance of being covered with hoar frost. His thin coat was no protection against the cold and his pants were so short that they showed six inches of cold, blue, stockingless leg between cuff and shoe. A sudden emotional explosion rocked me back to reality: "My God! All is NOT well with the world! Everybody's belly is not full! Not everyone is comfortable and happy!"

A few days before Christmas a cry for help came from an unexpected source. A police inspector called about a woman with a gun who was threatening suicide. The inspector had an extra-marital affair with this woman. He had given the gun to her "for protection." He called me to ask if I would handle the situation discreetly so that neither his wife nor the department would find out about his indiscretion.

I went to her room on Eddy Street, just off Mason, and found her living alone in a dingy hotel with a few shabby pieces of furniture. There was a hot plate on a small table, and several pictures of her four children thumb-tacked to the wall. Stuck in the corner of the mirror of her dresser, was the only Christmas card she had received last year. A few days before I saw her, the court had decided to put her children up for adoption. For the past several years, because of her drug and alcohol use, her children had been in foster homes, but she had visiting privileges. The lingering hope that perhaps she would one day have them back with her again had kept her going. From a crackling record player down the hall drifted the voice of Bing Crosby singing, "Have yourself a merry little Christmas." After some persuasion she gave me the gun. I spent a couple of hours with her and left her sitting on the edge of the bed, her hands clasped tightly on her lap, her knuckles white. Her chin was on her chest and tears were pouring down her cheeks. And that damned record player kept blaring, "Have yourself a merry little Christmas..."

I saw her regularly for several months following that initial meeting. I was able to get her into rehab for her alcoholism and drug use. Although I used to meet the inspector regularly at Sam's, I rarely saw him after this incident. The affair was casual and loveless for him, but filled with promise for her. In order to seduce her, he used the age-old line of a loveless, sexless marriage and his desire to get out of it. He had made promises of marriage as soon as he could get a divorce, promises he never intended to fulfill. But the prospect of marriage had filled her with new life and hope. It was the answer to her problems. She would have security and, most of all, she would have her children back! Now, she had nothing, not even a clandestine affair. I had a few contacts with her during the ensuing months but soon she disappeared from the neighborhood and I never heard from her again.

CHAPTER 12

Rage and Violence

Darkness, for many, is like a deadly mist creeping in from some mysterious enemy realm. Unfortunately, the darkness many battle is not from without, and the weapons they choose to fight it are totally ineffective. Their darkness is the darkness within, a darkness never confronted or checked. The darkness they never face is the Dark Night of the Soul and the weapons they choose to fight it are not effective

I was visiting with Johnny, my paper man friend when a young man carrying a broken umbrella ran by and said, pointing down a dark alley, "Looks like somebody got it." I ran through the darkness and found an old man, a wino, an outcast, a bum, dirty, unshaven and ragged. He had been a man once, once loving and once loved; now alone, broke and broken. I took his face in my hands and wiped away some of the blood. His face was slashed in a dozen places and he asked without expecting an answer, "Why did he do it Padre? Why did he hit me? I wasn't doin' nothin'. I was only sittin' in the doorway." A young man, probably the same one who pointed me down the alley, filled with demonic hatred found some animal satisfaction in beating this helpless and harmless old man. I was alone with him in the alley. It was dark. I was afraid, and filled with so much anger that I wanted to retch! The old man said, "Thanks, Padre. Say, can you spare some change?" I took him to Mission Emergency Hospital and, suddenly, the night was back to normal once more, although I'm not sure what the word "normal" means to describe the Tenderloin.

It was June 14, 1975. I found myself walking aimlessly down Turk Street and feeling a terrible loneliness myself. The night was dark, misty, and cold. My mind was absorbed with thoughts of the bloody old wino lying back in the dark and piss-filled doorway. A patrol officer stopped his car to tell me that he had just picked up a radio message saying that Theresa, a friend of mine, had been killed.

Many of my night friends were ordinary people doing ordinary things. However, each was unique if for no other reason than that they functioned at night and worked with a segment of the City population not seen or often ignored by daytime people. Theresa was one of these people. I never saw her during the day, nor did I see her wearing anything other than a faded pink dress covered by a frilly white apron tied around her waist. I can't say that we were good friends. But when night people see each other regularly, they become more than passing acquaintances. They are co-workers simply because of their shared working hours.

Theresa was a crusty bleached blond from the Bronx whose spicy vocabulary was belted out in a loud and abrasive accent. Yet under this façade was a caring and loving person, a being she made every attempt to hide. She never charged me for anything I ordered in her all-night restaurant on the corner of Leavenworth and Eddy streets. It catered to the toughest clientele in the City. The whole spectrum of the night population hung out in and around the place. But who a person was didn't matter to Theresa as much as what went on inside.

Prostitutes and pimps, pushers and heads, drag queens and winos, as well as clean-cut college kids looking for a good time in the City, found in Theresa a listening ear. She offered no maudlin sympathy, but would often give a hand out or a loan if the would-be recipient didn't try to con her. Her death was simple and senseless, like so many others in the Tenderloin. A man came in and ordered. He ate and tried to leave without paying. Theresa stopped him. He pulled out a gun and shot her—for a lousy buck forty-four.

Not all of the violence I observed was this senseless. Often it was drug

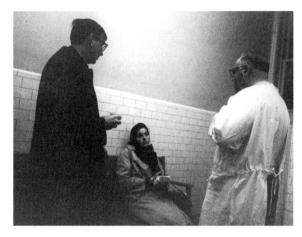

The night often took me to the Emergency Room.

induced. Much of it was a result of long-standing dysfunctional family relation-ships. Whatever the cause, hostility and death were always around the corner or just down the block in the Tenderloin: a tourist robbed in the middle of the intersection of Leavenworth and Turk; a drug pusher who got greedy and burned one too many clients thrown from the window of his sixth-floor hotel room on Turk Street, dying on the way to the hospital; a man who came to San Francisco to find work, and within the first ten minutes after his arrival, beaten and robbed of his nest egg. On Seventh Street, I stopped a pimp from beating one of his harem, a pregnant girl, and took her to the YMCA. She went into the ladies' room and jumped from the window twenty feet above the driveway to escape her pimp. I called an ambulance, but she lost her baby before she arrived at the Emergency Room.

Before I was well known on the street, I was met with hostility on the one hand and indifference on the other. Early one night, while I was locking my car door before hitting the streets, a young prostitute came up to me and wanted to talk. Almost immediately her pimp jumped out of a car parked across the street and came running over, yelling that I should stay away from his girls. He yanked me around and took a swing at me. Without thinking, I instinctively blocked his punch and swung with a right to his jaw. Luckily it landed. And so did he—on his rear end. He jumped up and ran away, hollering, "O.K., Father! O.K., Father!" I never saw him again. Somehow columnist Herb Caen picked up the incident from Hal Williams, the night clerk at the Y hotel and wrote in the *San Francisco Chronicle* of June 8, 1965:

> Rev. Donald E. Stuart, the Council of Churches' "Night Priest" (he covers the Tenderloin, Mission and North Beach) was swung on the other night by a baby giant panderer who thought he was muscling in. Rev. Stuart explained that he was only trying to save souls—and even a few heels.

Hostility directed toward me personally was rare, but it did happen. One time as I was going into Sam's HofBrau, a half dozen clean-cut young men from Riordan High School (a Catholic boys' school) mistook me for a Catholic priest. They stopped me and were cordial and friendly until I identified myself as a Protestant minister. Their initial politeness turned to hostility. A few days earlier a bombing in Northern Ireland, attributed to Protestants, had killed several Catholic school children. These high school kids were angry and rightfully so. But their anger was misdirected. They were pulling me toward the street where, I presumed, they intended to rough me up. Eddy, the bartender at Sam's, sensed something wrong, grabbed his shillelagh and came to my rescue. The boys scattered and that was the last I saw of them.

On another occasion, I pushed through a crowd in front of a gay bar to find eight policemen standing around a handcuffed young man curled up in a fetal position lying on the street. I recognized several of the policemen and one in particular who had the reputation for being brutal and homophobic. He was the one kicking the young man relentlessly. When I stepped into the circle of policemen, he ordered me to leave. I said nothing (I didn't dare open my mouth because of my own inner anger) but did not leave. Instead, we glared at each other until he blinked first and said, "Oh, the hell with it!" and walked away. Just my presence stopped the brutality.

Later that night, when I met several of the officers at a restaurant where we usually gathered after the bars closed, I asked why they just stood by and watched their fellow officer perform such a brutal act. With embarrassment one speaking for all of them, said, "Because one of these nights he might be my back up in a touch-and-go situation and I don't want to take an 'accidental' bullet in my back."

Kathleen, a regular caller, asked if I would meet her at the YMCA, which I did. She needed a few dollars to carry her through until her Supplemental Security Income check came. I had done this before and she was always faithful in paying me back. She had a sheaf of legal papers with her, which she insisted I read. She was a paranoid schizophrenic. Her documents reflected her condition. They rambled on without making much sense. Kathleen was especially agitated this night. She had met with a court-appointed attorney that morning. He said that he could not make sense of the accusations she was bringing against her ex-husband. After an hour of my trying to placate her and settle her down, my beeper went off.

I gave her the money she requested and started to leave. When I got up, she swore and screamed at me. She tore up the money I had given her. As I was walking across the lobby, she picked up a heavy glass ashtray and threw it at me. Fortunately, she missed. It hit the registration desk with a crash, leaving a dent, which remained a constant reminder of a close call.

Another close call came because of a request from a young divorcée who lived just a few blocks from my home in the Sunset District, although she was not aware that we were neighbors. Soon after I arrived, she made sexual overtures, which I, as gently as possible, refused. She had been recently divorced and was living alone with her two young children who were asleep in the bedroom. When I rejected her advances, she became belligerent and called me a fraud who "thought I was too good for her." (She somehow thought the Night Ministry was a wry name for a "call-boy" service.) As I was making a fumbling attempt to get out of the double-bolted front door, she threw a table lamp at me. When the lamp reached the end of the electric cord, it snapped at the base and sent sparks flying throughout the living room, which startled her back to reality. She mumbled some awkward apology, after which I was much relieved to get to my car and head for home. She had been terribly hurt by her ex-husband. On this night, she was especially lonely. It was their fifth wedding anniversary. It was just another rejection by "those miserable pigs called men."

Sometimes, face-to-face with violence almost every night, I had to work to curb the violence I felt within myself. Once I totally lost my cool and handled a situation with a violent outburst of my own.

Ray, the security guard at the Greyhound bus depot, was always sensitive to people he thought I could help. About midnight one night he called me to pick up Aaron, a thirteen-year-old runaway from his conservative Mormon family in Utah. His parents were more restrictive than he thought he could tolerate. His fair skin and shock of tight blond curls made him look like a classic Botticelli angel. I worked to persuade him to allow me to call his parents for permission to care for him for a few days. Without that permission, he would end up in Juvenile Hall where he would undoubtedly be physically and sexually abused.

Aaron asked if he could use the men's room. Ray went with him into the waiting room and directed him upstairs. When he was gone longer than I thought he should be, I went looking for him. The men's room appeared empty but I did hear a stifled cry and gagging sound coming from one of the booths. I looked under the door and saw a configuration of feet that looked suspicious. I kicked the door in and found a large man trying to shove his penis into Aaron's mouth. I felt a rage such as I had never felt before and with a strength I didn't know I had, grabbed the man by his belt and pulled him from the booth. The momentum caught him off balance and he went flying across the room landing under a row of washbasins along the opposite wall. He swore and yelled at me to "mind my own fucking business." He started to get up, still holding the knife he used to threaten and subdue Aaron. He was twice my size and his face was contorted with anger and rage. Before he could lunge at me, I kicked him in the groin with all my strength. He grunted and fell to his knees. He tried to get up, still holding the knife. I kicked him in the face splattering blood over the room. He crumpled to the floor. This time he didn't even try to get up. The noise alerted Ray who came running into the room and within a few minutes the police were there to haul the man off to jail.

Thirty years have passed but the event still haunts me. Basically I am a man of peace and have preached peace all of my life. This experience was a good lesson to me: I, too, could lose control and express rage to the extent that, if I had not knocked the man unconscious, I might have killed him. Still, I do not regret doing what I did when I consider what could have happened to this innocent young boy if I had not intervened. I took Aaron home with me. He slept on our dining room floor until the next day when I could make arrangements to get him back to Utah.

I never heard from Aaron after he reached home but I doubt that he even considered running away again.

CHAPTER 13

The Haight-Ashbury

S an Francisco, like the Siren Lorelei on the banks of the Rhine, lured her lovers from all parts of the world, some of them to their death. This was especially true during the 1960s when the Haight-Ashbury district enticed the flower children to "come to San Francisco with a flower in your hair." Her call was universally alluring. During the "Summer of Love" in 1967, an estimated 100,000 young people crowded into Haight-Ashbury.

Some came to find fame and fortune, only to leave disillusioned and shocked by the City's indifference and coldness. These pilgrims to a promised land came from small towns all over America. The children of Europe also heard the haunting words of the song "San Francisco," and they too came like lemmings to the sea. They were enchanted by the Great Lady's glamour and promise only to find her just as dingy, just as lonely, and just as much a captive of urbanization as the places they had hoped to escape.

Many came bringing with them a talent, which may have been appreciated in their hometown, but was nothing compared to the competition they faced in the Bay Area. They found the glamour a façade that quickly wore thin. They went hungry, homeless, and friendless in the City that they found much colder, in every way, than they had anticipated. The freedom they sought from parents and restrictive communities was soon traded for slavery to sex and drugs. Many were simply destroyed. The hypnotizing notes of this Piper of the West, heard in all parts of our nation and, in fact, in all parts of the world, enticed young and old alike to a Utopia which never existed.

Night after night they called. Night after night they came, each with his or her unique story. Yet they were woven together by a strange sameness:

"I was hitch-hiking. When we stopped for gas I went to the rest room but when I came out, my ride had taken off with everything I owned!"

"I met this great chick in the Haight. She said she'd watch my things while I made a phone call. When I came back, everything was gone."

"I came to Frisco to get a job, but man, there's nothing here! So I've got to hustle (prostitute myself) to make enough bread for room and board."

In the mid-1960s, the war in Vietnam was escalating. Dissent was picking up momentum among the hippies moving into the Haight-Asbury. They brought with them a political agenda that found expression in demonstrations and near riots. Discontent was showing up at almost every university across the country.

The University of California at Berkeley became infamous as the birthplace of class disruption and demonstration. Mario Savio and his Free Speech Movement spread swiftly to the other schools in the University system and then across the country. Since many Haight residents were San Francisco State students (where S. I. Hayakawa, then President of San Francisco State, was holding a hard line against dissidents), demonstrations moved into the Haight-Ashbury district as well.

The Haight-Ashbury neighborhood of San Francisco was a Victorian "village" in the center of the City. It surrounded the Panhandle, that narrow extension of Golden Gate Park reaching east from Stanyan Street for several blocks. The architecture was a mix of beautiful middle-class Victorian homes, a few large mansions and a scattering of apartment buildings dating back to the

Head shop on Haight Street.

1920s. Haight Street, two blocks south of the Panhandle, was a straight commercial district with traditional stores, such as Woolworth's. The neighborhood even boasted of its own movie house, the Haight Theater. There was a small town atmosphere about the area with a closely-knit merchants' organization that vehemently resisted the changes taking place in their neighborhood.

In the late 1950s and early '60s, Caltrans planned to extend a freeway from the Bay Bridge through the center of Golden Gate Park that would have meant the destruction of the Panhandle. The merchants and residents alike mounted a campaign that stirred the City Council to vote against the freeway.

Many of the Victorian houses, built when families were large, were divided into apartments. Rents were cheap, and living in the Haight was convenient to transportation, the park, the museums, and the band shell. It was a great area for San Francisco State University students to both live and hang out. The park was a perfect place to meet and make friends, and an especially great place to get high. There were a few all-night eateries, like Bob's and the House of Do-Nuts, and even a couple of gay bars.

Then a little shop called the Psychedelic Shop opened on the corner of Haight and Ashbury streets and life changed in the Haight. The shop, so important to the newly-arriving Hippies, was probably the reason the names of the cross streets came to designate the entire neighborhood. It was the first store to bring together books and paraphernalia pertinent to the whole psychedelic drug culture. Ironically, the shop was opened by natives of the neighborhood, whose father managed the traditional, straight Woolworth's 5 & 10 just down the street.

It became a popular hang out, not only because of the paraphernalia it sold, but also because it was the ticket outlet for the many concerts being performed in the Bay Area. The most important reason why the shop became a gathering place was that the proprietors did not eject those who had no intention of buying anything. This "obstructing the sidewalk" became a problem with the straight residents who eventually won a petition to have the shop closed.

Just visiting the shop was a trip in itself. It was jammed full of every psychedelic poster printed, every bit of drug paraphernalia produced, a large assortment of occult books and the latest in clothing appropriate to the acid head style-conscious. It also carried the most complete selection of Zigzag posters available anywhere.

Soon older established businesses started closing and moving out, leaving room for shops more sympathetic to San Francisco State students and the rapidly swelling numbers of flower children. One of the new businesses was the Drugstore Cafe, on the corner of Haight and Masonic. It was decorated to look like an old, established apothecary, but it was in reality a traditional coffee house. The police didn't appreciate the implications of the name so they pressured the owners to change it. They did—to "The Drogstore."

I often stopped at the Drogstore for breakfast or my last cup of coffee for the night on my way home at five or six o'clock in the morning. One morning, I was sitting at the long plank-like table facing Haight Street, next to a young teenager. He told me of his leaving home somewhere in the East Bay because his mother had recently remarried after divorcing his father. He didn't like his new stepfather, and evidently the feeling was mutual.

He was a sweet, naive kid who didn't belong alone in an area like this. He was wearing an interesting ring with the bas-relief features of Caesar encircled with diamonds. When I commented on the ring, he, without hesitation, took it off and insisted that I have it. I found this gesture common among these beautiful, gentle young people who found their way to San Francisco in the early days of the Hippie movement. Although he said he was glad to be on his own, it was obvious that he was scared and lonely. We arranged to meet again, and continued to do so over a period of several months. I was able to find a safe place for him to live. With his permission, I called his mother and, without revealing his location, was able to help them work through some of their differences. Before he left the Haight to go home, I returned his ring as a symbol of the circle of friendship it represented. Several months later he called to tell me that he was back in school and that his home life had greatly improved.

On another occasion I was called to an apartment building on Fell Street near Fillmore. The caller said a kid he had picked up a couple of days before was on the roof of the five-story building threatening to jump. I went to the roof and after some time, talked the boy down. He was seventeen years old and had recently come to the City from the desert. He had lived there in a tent with his father since his mother died five years earlier. His father had turned him on to pot when he was only twelve years old. When he came to the City, he was open to experimenting with harder stuff. That particular night he had dropped acid and his difficulty with hallucinations was compounded by the theft of his beloved guitar. I persuaded him to have something to eat. After several hours of talk, he came down enough from both the roof and his trip to agree to allow me to get a room for him at the YMCA. This was only after I was able to persuade him that I wasn't going to take him home for sex, which happened to him regularly since he arrived in the City. Even though he was pretty much through his bad trip, he was still afraid to stay in the room alone. He asked if I would stay with him, which I did. I tucked him in like a small boy and sat by his bed, holding his hand until he fell asleep.

He had promised to see me the next day so that we could visit some pawnshops to find another guitar. But he checked out early and I never saw him again.

Many of the young people migrating to San Francisco were the children of World War II veterans who were determined that their children would not experience the hardships they had experienced, and could not understand why their children refused to jump at the opportunities offered them. The fathers had earned an education through the GI Bill, an education not possible to them before the war. But the decision to take advantage of that education was still theirs to make and they were influential in charting their own course of life. These fathers would say to their children, "You don't know how lucky you are, I never had the opportunities you have." But the children sensed a hypocrisy that alienated them from their veteran fathers who supported a "wrong" war in Vietnam and could not understand their children's lack of patriotism.

There was a breakdown of family life, which the parents didn't recognize. There was a lack of structure on which these children could model their lives. Many of the parents had married in haste before being sent overseas. When the men returned from the war, some returned as strangers to their wives. Their marriages started falling apart. The economy was good so both mothers, who discovered an independence not offered them before the war, and fathers worked long hours to provide their children with all the material advantages which they, the parents, had not enjoyed at a comparable age. Their children often felt abandoned, manipulated, and neglected. Some parents abused alcohol and popped pills to give them a high, then others to bring them down.

It was not unusual for parents to tell me that they always had alcohol available for their teenage children so that they wouldn't be tempted to try "harder stuff." The parents refused to admit that alcohol and diet pills and sleeping pills were just as addictive as the drugs their kids could buy on the street. Their permissiveness and lack of structure simply strengthened their children's feelings of abandonment. The children felt that their parents didn't care what happened to them. This sowed the seeds of anger and rage, which came to full bloom when these young people left home. In many instances the parents were more relieved than troubled when their children did leave. The children, with long hair (the "bad" influence of the Beatles) and beards (if they could grow one) and strange clothes styles, were an embarrassment to the parents in their suburban homes and country-club living. If their child was also gay along with being a drug-using "head," he or she was not only allowed to leave home, but was encouraged to do so.

The rage of the children continued to grow until it sometimes reached explosive proportions. If these pseudo Hippies continued to live at home, they experienced rejection and ridicule from their peers at school and even from their friends at church. The chasm between their lifestyle and the straight community grew wider and wider. They heard the luring lyrics of the songs encouraging them to join the "Summer of Love." They came to the City in great numbers and few parents tried to stop them. This enraged their children all the more.

Some military-trained fathers laid high, arbitrary expectations on their children and made life decisions for them without consultation. Because of the hypocrisy of alcoholic, pill-popping parents, the feeling of abandonment through divorce and different lifestyles, the off-handed rejection of their alternate life choices, the children sought some form of community that would provide them with support. They rejected marriage; living together was the accepted norm. They were ripe prey for gurus and vulnerable to cults.

By 1966, the Haight-Ashbury was well established as the Hippie center of the world. Young people by the hundreds were migrating to the area and the face of the district was changing rapidly.

Even the venerable Haight Theater went through a metamorphosis. It was unable to make it as a traditional movie house in the midst of a not-so-traditional neighborhood, so it switched to showing gay flicks. When that proved unprofitable, it became an Assembly of God church. That, too, failed, and the theater stood empty until an attorney brother team bought it, changed its name to the Straight Theater and converted it into a community center large enough for dances, light shows, and performing groups.

The Haight-Ashbury was not only the social and cultural center of the Northern California psychedelic community, but also its economic capital in the one business that mattered: the drug market.

Dealing marijuana was the economic base of the Haight-Asbury hippie community. Nearly every hippie sold a little grass, and many didn't know any other way of making a living. The Beats had smoked grass and dealt it too—since there was no legal distribution system. Most potheads had sold as well as bought from time to time—but in their time the grass market was small. Even their language of dealing was diminutive, ten dollars being called a dime and five dollars a nickel, as Charles Perry described in his book, *The Haight Ashbury*.

Marijuana was by far the most popular drug being used both by the Hippies moving into San Francisco and on the college campuses in the early 1960s when I began my work as Night Minister. As the demand grew, pushing pot became a "home industry" with more and more street kids dealing in order to make a few bucks, as well as to satisfy their own demands.

This quickly began to change as more professional drug dealers recognized the profits to be realized by the expansion of the market to include more expensive, hard stuff, and the face of the Hippie movement began to deteriorate. Popping a few buds and smoking a few joints kept the participants mellow, but with the introduction of harder drugs like acid (LSD), speed, and cocaine, paranoia and bad trips resulted in permanent altered states of consciousness and even death. The preaching of psychedelic drug advocate Timothy Leary to "tune in, turn on, drop out" did little to improve the attitude of the straight community toward the hippies, even though his influence on the young hippies in the Haight-Ashbury was minimal.

In the middle of 1965, as Charles Perry wrote in *The Haight Ashbury*:

>...while marijuana was still in its seasonal short supply, there was more LSD than anybody wanted. The price of a tab of acid had fallen to $1 and under as demand dried up. Haight Street was speed street now, which they used as freely as tranquilizers or barbiturates to overcome the feeling of depression that followed a week-long sleepless "speed run" of Methadone-fueled activity. If they became junkies they became thieves, but as speeders they were physically dangerous. After a couple of days without sleep they started to "space," to fall into moments of unconsciousness while physiologically awake. Speed freaks developed hallucinations, as if the mind were struggling to dream in the absence of sleep. These hallucinations tended to be paranoid and violent.

In 1964, when I first began my work in the Haight, I had no qualms about answering a call to the area or in wandering the streets on a slow night. But as hard drugs, especially speed (with its accompanying paranoia) became more prevalent, my phone-line volunteers were instructed to call either my associate, Chuck Lewis, or the police if I didn't check with them within an hour. Fortunately, even though I was surrounded by a considerable amount of danger and rage (which often was not understood even by the perpetrators of that rage), and experienced some difficult counseling situations with heads on a high, I was never seriously threatened or in danger in the Haight.

The years 1964 and 1965 saw a great migration of hippies and wannabe hippies move into the Haight-Ashbury. After a few months of going hungry and being alone on the City streets, they discovered they got no more support from their fellow street "friends" than they received at home. Some became involved in some form of communal living. Some were sexually abused by older acquaintances and had even their meager possessions repeatedly ripped off. Their rage often found expression in paranoia, mistrust and violence. It was not unusual to see these once loving "flower children" become exploiters themselves. They, too, would mistreat the weaker, stealing their shoes, a piece of clothing, or the few dollars they might be carrying.

There were situations in which I could predict the inevitable conclusion resulting from the use of speed, but I felt totally helpless in slowing the momentum toward self-destruction or even in showing a detour. Once, while on an early morning walk on Haight near Stanyan, I was approached by a clean cut kid who had recently come to the City from a small town in the Midwest. Billy said he was seventeen, but he looked much younger. He made an attempt to look hip, but failed. He wore bell bottomed jeans and a clean white shirt; his hair was combed and he was clean-shaven, primarily because he couldn't yet grow a beard. He had been in the City long enough to make some contacts. He had a place to crash, but was on his own when it came to finding something to eat. He had trouble panhandling.

I took him to Bob's for breakfast, which gave us an opportunity to talk. He said his father was a college history professor who was "always trying to impress somebody." He thought his father was too strict with him and his younger brother. He said his mother was more interested in church and social organizations than she was in her family, so he doubted she even realized that he was gone. Billy was pleasant, polite, articulate, and charming. He was not yet caught up in the political agenda and rhetoric prevalent on the street at that time. He hardly knew that Vietnam existed, let alone being prepared to protest against our involvement there.

We met a few more times after that initial contact, just to talk and eat. He was always hungry! He seemed genuinely anxious to be with me and said he appreciated our conversation because "you listen to what I have to say." After a while he trusted me enough to invite me back to his "squat" on Frederick Street.

From the outside it was just another abandoned building with boarded-up windows and doors. Billy led me around to the rear where he swung back a loose sheet of plywood and we squeezed through a narrow opening into a fetid room. Since there was no running water in the house, this room had become their toilet. He held my hand as he led me through the debris toward the front of the house and into a room littered with musty smelling sleeping bags and foul smelling blankets. A few candles and an old camp lantern lighted the room.

Billy introduced me to his eight or ten friends, none older than twenty. We sat in a circle on the floor, rapping, in this "shooting gallery" (so named as a place where people shared drugs and/or needles for injecting drugs). Out of nowhere a syringe appeared filled with speed. One by one they took a hit, licked the needle and passed it on. They respected my refusal. Surprisingly, they were eager to talk about their plans and hopes for the future. Some of their dreams were realistic while others seemed to stem from the hallucinations. But all of these young people had dreams. My fear was that drugs would soon deaden those dreams, or worse, that these youngsters would die searching for dreams that were mere fantasies.

I saw Billy a few more times, and then he disappeared. I went back to his squat in an attempt to find out something about him, but it was in the process of being cleaned up and renovated. He had talked to me of the possibly of moving back home, but whether he did or not I don't know. Did he see the squalor in which he was living to be far from the romantic lyrics he listened to before he came to the Haight? Was he able to see what speed was doing to him and his friends, or did he end up a John Doe on a slab in the city morgue? During the height of the hippie movement an average of fifty kids a day were buried in unmarked graves across the country.

Many of the young people migrating to the Haight-Ashbury from all parts of the world were following a Pied Piper whose music they couldn't quite decipher. They looked for love, but soon discovered that free sex didn't equate with love. The sex became wild and ribald, but lacked the intimacy they were seeking. Pot was fun and seemingly harmless, but they soon moved on to harder stuff, which fried their brains and left them with more problems than they had before they had come to this hippie haven. It was not surprising that many of these gentle, seriously searching young people were lured into cults or listened to the seductive voices of a variety of gurus.

What was surprising is that these same young people who left home to escape a "restrictive society" and to get out from under parental authority now embraced a regimentation they would have resented from their teachers or parents. The sex they believed to be the epitome of the good life soon faded and they entered groups that were almost convent-like with stringent rules and regulations demanding celibacy.

The Hare Krishnas were those shaven-headed, saffron-robed, chanting young people. They were ubiquitous on street corners and airports. They offered some sense of serenity and stability to many of the young people coming to the City who were soon burned out by the Haight-Ashbury scene. The offer of clean lodgings and regular meals was appealing to many who had gone hungry for days and without a shower for weeks. The chanting mantras and demanding spiritual disciplines gave them a religious experience not offered by old-line Churches. Also, the fact that this new direction bugged their parents was no small reason for many to follow a non-traditional path.

The Universal Life Church, the "Moonies," was a fast-growing, worldwide church headed by a charismatic Korean preacher named Rev. Sun Myung Moon. Their evangelists saturated bus depots, airports, street corners, and hangouts of any kind appealing to young people. They lured them with promises of food, dance, and congenial company in order to plant the seeds of conversion.

It was not unusual for me to meet such recruits, either young men or women, like David, a teenaged sailor I ran into in an all night restaurant. He had just come from one of the "Moonie" meetings where he had been lured by the promise of food and companionship with a hint of sex. He went to the meeting where he got only the food, spiced with a goodly portion of Moonie rhetoric.

Bob was a high-school senior who was working on a fishing boat for the summer. His boat was damaged in a storm and was in port being repaired. This gave him some shore time to enjoy the City. He accidentally came across me in Sam's restaurant and ended up spending a considerable amount of time with me on my beat. One day he was picked up by a beautiful young Asian girl. She was proselytizing for the Moonies at the Powell Street BART station. He went with her to her apartment thinking that they were going to be alone. Instead, it was crowded with Moonie workers and the young men and women they had contacted during the day. He was persuaded to join them at their retreat center in Sonoma County. While there he was deprived of sleep, nourishing food, and, particularly, privacy until he was "converted," but still capable of fostering doubts and reservations.

On one of their excursions into the City, he slipped away and immediately got in touch with me. This once bright-eyed, vivacious, intelligent young man was almost unrecognizable. His answers to my questions were monosyllabic. His attention span was minimal and his self esteem non-existent. I saw him almost nightly for several months, during which time he began to recover some of his original joie de vivre. I was able to return him to his home in another state where he began a slow recovery with the help of a counselor who specialized in working with ex-cult members.

One of the most difficult obstacles that Bob had to overcome was the feeling of "How could I have been so stupid? What was wrong with my mind in the first place to allow this to happen to me?" He kept in touch with me for several years and gradually returned to his old self. He married his high school girlfriend and fathered a son. But always in the back of his mind was the memory of a very black period in his life, which was never totally resolved.

The Farm was another movement, which, though it had its origins at San Francisco State, had considerable influence on the students living in the Haight-Asbury, since so many students lived there.

It began at the height of the college turbulence when Stephen Gaskin, a teacher and favored disciple of S.I. Hayakawa at San Francisco State who was headed for a successful academic career, dropped out. He took a lot of drugs, then gave up the drugs and began to lecture on how to get naturally high, how to live high without LSD. He wasn't selling any packaged religious principles, just a search for a new way of life. The lectures and open discussions that evolved from his writing class, called Monday Night Class, were attended by more than five hundred people in San Francisco. Many of the same people ended up with Gaskin in Tennessee on "The Farm."

Gaskin gathered students, professionals and hippies who were searching for an alternative lifestyle. The younger ones were rebelling against what they considered too much parental control and traditional religious values. He persuaded them to outfit old school buses, painted in psychedelic style, and to travel across the country in a hippie caravan.

Although Gaskin was a charismatic guru in many ways, his goal was not total obedience to him or mind control as it was with the Moonies, or later on with Jim Jones in his Peoples Temple. He did not advocate mind-altering drug use as Timothy Leary did, and did not advocate free sex. Premarital sex was not encouraged and extramarital sex was anathema. Children were honored and respected and close family ties were adhered to within communal living. Birth control was not practiced, so even before they left San Francisco, their numbers expanded.

Eventually in Tennessee, this group pooled their money, bought land and settled down to communal living as vegetarians, raising and eating soybeans, living modestly, and smoking a little pot (which they called their "sacrament"). They continue to thrive and are considered one of the most successful communes coming out of the hippie era.

In my latter days in the Night Ministry, I felt a sadness watching the decline of the Haight-Ashbury. It began simply and beautifully by young people looking for some semblance of order and love in a world moving through the confusion and destruction of World War II and the high prosperity of a nation bursting at the seams as it expanded to develop and buy more and more "things." The ex-World War II servicemen, the parents of the hippies, were working hard to give their children all the luxuries they thought they were deprived of in their youth. They gave their children everything except the one thing they really wanted: themselves. These children came to the Haight with lofty dreams and high hopes, which often skirted reality. The world they were looking for didn't exist, even in their drug-induced dreams. They soon discovered that their Utopia was not to be found in the Haight. By the time they made this discovery, many had reached the point of no return. The consequences of their choices were disastrous. Fortunately, the majority walked away with a trunk full of memories and a lifetime full of experiences.

I am still in touch with some of these "flower children" and, although they seem to be back in the mainstream of our culture, there is a different attitude, an aura that sets them apart. They started on a journey back in the 1950s and '60s that has not been completed, and perhaps never should be. They are still looking for ways to make their lives more loving and meaningful.

CHAPTER 14

My Parish of the Past

*I believe that we have reached the time when we must put aside
our self-protective type of religion with its careful exclusions and
respectable cliques and must recognize both Christ and ourselves
in the most disreputable members of society.*

—Episcopal Bishop James Pike

As I began work on this book, I discovered that I had to struggle to dredge up some memories about my work on the streets between 1964 and 1976, memories of events long since past and long since experienced. I found myself surprised by how deeply I had buried many situations that I once thought I could never forget. I also was surprised by how many wounds were still festering and going unhealed. It has been good to touch those wounds once more so that they can find the healing brought on by new experiences, new perspectives, and new growth.

It is likely that many of those reading this book may have been involved in the traditional, institutional Church. Unfortunately, too often the institution has been too busy with the task of self-perpetuation, and catering to those whose allegiance would be an asset. The outpouring, self-sacrificing nature of the Church has been piously talked about, but often practiced only in terms of life within the structure, not in terms of the Church in relation to the world.

During my last nights on the street, knowing that they were numbered, I reflected on the changes that had taken place, not only in the Tenderloin, but in myself as well. I walked the streets with a different feeling than I once had. The initial fear of the "roughest, toughest section of the city" was long since gone. This was my territory now—my turf. These were my streets. The faces I passed were not the faces of strangers. They were not enemies to be feared, but friends who turned to me in times of trouble and to whom I could turn in an emergency. They were my congregation. I was at home there and I was at ease with these so-called outcasts of society. But the scene had changed during those twelve years.

Once the streets were filled with people, some were well-dressed suburbanites enjoying the excitement of a night on the town. Others were the night people, doing their thing in the only section of the City that, in the words of Herb Caen, "didn't know how to raise its eyebrows." Night sounds echoed and re-echoed out of the bars and off the buildings, which throbbed with the life within them. After-hours clubs were packed with those determined to fill every moment in "Everybody's Favorite City" with as much life and excitement as possible. All-night restaurants were always full, and the real shows were not in the nightclubs, but on the street corners. The Black Hawk, the Square Chair, the Round Table, Coffee Ron's, and Chuckers are names out of the past that are now barely remembered. Nothing has taken their place—and perhaps nothing should.

Some of the people and places are better gone. Some were ripoffs; some were dangerous. Some I miss with certain nostalgia. What happened to my parish of the past, the aged who could be found on the streets at any hour of the night? They aren't gone. They haven't been relocated. Now they sit in fear behind barricaded doors and shade-drawn windows, alone, and waiting, waiting.

The streets have changed. The City Fathers are proud of the "clean-up." The police brag about a "reduction in crime." But if this is true, why is there so much fear? Why do more and more people eye me suspiciously? Why are the streets so barren? Where have all the people gone? The shopkeepers and restaurant owners who complained about people loitering near their doorways had them arrested or run off. And now they are gone. And the shops and restaurants are closed. Litter fills the doorways, and drunks with whiskey-shaking hands light up a butt, only to quickly blow out the match in order to hide their shame in the darkness.

Don leaving his parish.

The street-canyons still reverberate with city sounds, but somehow the sounds are hollow. They are ghostly echoes of people who once were, but are no more. The hippie is a part of history. The servicemen are gone. The aged cringe behind locked doors. The wide-eyed tourists and conventioneers pace the streets, eagerly searching the faces of what turn out to be only other tourists and conventioneers looking for the same San Francisco adventure.

Twelve years on the streets of the Tenderloin! Twelve years of being jolted into action by my beeper. Twelve years of responding to suicide calls, of listening to heartache, of comforting the discomforted.

I wrote my last report of the Night Ministry sitting in our son's apartment on top of Nob Hill. This gave me a bird's eye view of the Tenderloin, my parish for so long. From that perspective the Tenderloin looked almost inviting and beautiful. "Almost," because I could not be satisfied with a surface impression. I could not help but ruminate on those past years, which called up from the depth of my memories thousands of experiences and an equal number of people who touched my life and in some way changed it, as I hope I touched and changed theirs.

To my right I looked down on Twin Peaks and just beyond them, the huge lighted (at that time) cross of Mt. Davidson. The fog billowed and swirled over their crests and began to roll down their sides like a voracious beast devouring everything in its path.

Although I had seen it a hundred times, I was still left breathless by the sight of the City nestled beneath me. The firefly lights twinkled in silent symphony, the neon signs flashed their majestic montage, the yellow lights of the bridges reached out like the arms of a loving mother—all gave the impression of peace and tranquility. How could there possibly be trouble in a city so breathtaking? How, in the face of such beauty, could people flaunt their troubles and be concerned with the mundane problems of living?

I left the apartment and walked down California Street. I stopped at L'Etoile to say "Hi" (and good-bye) to pianist Peter Minton, and then on to the

Mark Hopkins to listen to keyboardist Bob Moonan. I didn't expect trouble nor did I look for it in either of these rooms filled with flashing diamonds, swirling minks and black ties. But I knew that even here I would catch empty eyes and shallow smiles. Even here, someone would corner me to share some intimacy, some concern, some hope that had been brooding inside, waiting for a listening ear.

I started down the steep hill on Mason Street and headed for the Tenderloin, only a few blocks away but a world apart from the splendor on Nob Hill. Nostalgic, I began to recap my years on the street. Yet, how is it possible to cover fifty thousand calls in a few short blocks? Some of those calls blended together in an unrecognizable blur. So many people entered and left my life so quickly that they have become little more than a statistic. Some I remember all too well, and would just as soon forget. Others, like twinkling stars in a stormy sky, have touched my life and helped give it direction.

I remembered my first nights filled with fear. It was not so much a fear for my personal safety (though there was some of that too) but more a fear of my own inability to handle crises. Could I stem the flow of blood and life from someone who had slashed his or her wrists? Would I be able to say the right things to someone determined to kill him- or herself? Would I be able to give hope where there was no hope? These questions troubled me all through my ministry and sent a surge of adrenaline rushing through my body every time my beeper went off.

The Night Ministry has never left me. Twenty-five years later I think of those years as the high point of my entire ministry. I am still warmed by the memory of innumerable friendships that strengthened and sustained and entertained me. Every time I hear "Send in the Clowns" or "Cabaret" I cannot help but remember the resonant, incomparable tones of Annie Farrell who, for years, sang in the many clubs in the Tenderloin and on Polk Street. Hearing "What I Did for Love" still brings a tear to my eye. I recall the many others who were my "assistants" without even knowing it: Johnny, at the paper stand in front of the Bus Depot; Hal Williams, the Night Manager at the Turk Street YMCA, and Bernie Haines at the Golden Gate Y who has remained a life-long friend.

It is said that pain is not long remembered and the distasteful soon forgotten. I am not certain I believe that to be true for all situations. It surely does not apply to the years I spent in the Night Ministry. Although I retired more than twenty years ago, some of the experiences are just as vivid and just as painful now as they were the nights on which they occurred. I wonder whether I would have been so eager to accept the position if I could have foreseen just how traumatic some of the encounters would be. Perhaps I was just as innocent and naive as the young Hippies I met in the Haight Ashbury.

Yet in retrospect, I can say, without equivocation, that I would do it again and can affirm that my years in the Night Ministry were the richest and most rewarding of my fifty years in the ministry.

Devoted spouses Eunice R. Stuart (1923–2008) and Donald E. Stuart (1922–2014) posed for this portrait in 1966.

LIGHTEN THE DARKNESS, REKINDLE THE HOPE

This 50th Anniversary edition of *I'm Listening as Fast as I Can* honors the early work of the Night Ministry in Don Stuart's own words and augments his vivid memoir. It profiles the four Night Ministers who have served since 1964, describes the current scope of Night Ministry programs, and presents a timeline highlighting events in the Night Ministry's history.

SAN FRANCISCO
NIGHT MINISTRY
50 YEAR ANNIVERSARY 1964-2014

Camaraderie and warmth abounded when the unique fraternity of four Night Ministers met to reminisce in Claremont, CA in 2011. *From left:* Don Fox, Don Stuart, Chuck Lewis, and Lyle Beckman.

THE FOUR NIGHT MINISTERS

BY SANDRA GARY

Only four people have served as The Night Minister from the Night Ministry's beginning in 1964 to its 50th anniversary in 2014. The Reverends Donald E. Stuart of the United Church of Christ, Charles H. Lewis of the Lutheran Church in America, Donald A. Fox, of The Episcopal Church, and Lyle J. Beckman of the Evangelical Lutheran Church in America comprise this unique fraternity. Representing different denominations, they have developed and built upon a single approach to ministering to people at nighttime: offering compassionate, non-judgmental care, counsel, crisis intervention, and referrals.

It takes a special kind of person to want to work with people who are needy or in crisis in the middle of the night. It takes courage, creativity and conviction to carry a ministry of listening love and pastoral presence into the night, onto the streets, and through the receiver of a telephone. In 50 years, the Night Ministry has never missed a single night helping and listening from the hours of 10:00 p.m. to 4:00 a.m. Here are profiles of these dedicated pastors who have collectively offered hope and brought comfort in the middle of the night to hundreds of thousands of grateful souls.

PHOTO BY TOM JELICK

THE REV. DONALD E. STUART 1964–1976

I n the early 1960s, the Summer of Love was a future happening, and lyricist John Phillips had not quite yet written the words, "If you're going to San Francisco, be sure to wear some flowers in your hair..." thus inspiring thousands of young people to flock to San Francisco. Yet the streets of our city were already filling up with young runaways, gay refugees, and a burgeoning population of newly arriving rootless people of all stripes.

This trend of rootless people on the street, some homeless, and some turning to drugs and prostitution, did not go unobserved by the Protestant denominations of the city. Seven members of the interdenominational Council of Churches got together to sponsor an experimental ministry to reach out to "street people" at night. They placed ads to attract a pastor to minister to these "night people."

The name of the Rev. Donald Stuart was submitted as a candidate for the job. Then serving as a United Church of Christ pastor in Lincoln, Nebraska, Don was offered the job, answered the call, started work in September, and launched the experimental ministry on November 1, 1964. His annual salary was $6,000 with a housing allowance of $1,800.

He served until 1976, becoming the beloved founder of the Night Ministry in San Francisco, which remains the longest running such organization in the country. Apart from police, fire, and ambulance services, the Night Ministry continues to be the only organization in San Francisco offering face-to-face counseling and intervention to people in crisis in the middle of the night.

March 28, 1922 to March 5, 2014

Born on March 28, 1922 in Chicago, IL, Don Stuart graduated from college at Elmhurst College in Elmhurst, IL, near Chicago and from Mission House Seminary in Sheboygan, WI, in 1950. He served two years in the Navy from 1944 to 1946, during which time he was stationed on Treasure Island and fell in love with San Francisco. That made it easy for him to accept the call to serve the experimental ministry initiated by the Council of Churches.

After the Night Ministry, Don went on to be the Pastor of St. John's United Church of Christ in San Francisco, serving from 1977 to 1987. He also lent his passion and talents for working with young people, to help found Larkin Street Youth Services.

He retired to Pilgrim Place in Claremont, CA, in 1990 and was active for many years in civic efforts of Claremont, including serving on the Human Services Commission, and the Claremont Gang Prevention Task Force.

He died peacefully, surrounded by family, in Claremont on March 5, 2014. His survivors include his son, the Rev. Mark Stuart of Hollywood, CA, and daughter Kathleen Stuart of South Lake Tahoe, CA, and grandchildren Monique Boyer and Andre Boyer. His beloved wife Eunice died in 2008.

In a conversation among the four Night Ministers in 2011, Don Stuart remembered what life was like for Eunice and himself during his Night Ministry years:

> I would come home usually about six or seven o'clock in the morning. In fact, I was going to title my book, *The Bed was Never Made*, because it never was. I would get into bed as Eunice was getting up. Then she would get the kids ready for school and get breakfast ready for them and I would crawl into bed and sleep then until four thirty or five o'clock in the evening. I'd get up in time for them to get home from school and we would have dinner together. Evenings were as much as I could do until ten o'clock.

I tried to do as much together as a family as we would do if we were a normal family. I tried to make school and church events that a family would do together. I would arrange for rides home for them or leave early enough to get them home before I went to work. I don't think she ever stayed to the end of anything we scheduled. She always managed to get the children home at a decent hour.

Eunice and I were very compatible as far as I was concerned. We never had any arguments and we rarely disagreed on subjects that were unimportant—or important—to us. Our children were always part of our family planning and decisions. We had a very good family relationship.

We had as normal a life as it was possible to get. I went to church a lot more than many of the members did, and taught Sunday School. So I don't think my private life was altered too much by my involvement with the Night Ministry.

Don Stuart's successors remain devoted to the founding Night Minister. They share some fond memories:

On a Barstool

Chuck Lewis, the Second Night Minister, went out with Don Stuart on the first night of the experimental ministry, not knowing where to go or what to expect. Chuck describes one of Don's encounters in the earliest days in the Tenderloin, when people wearing clerical collars were usually out to proselytize, shame, or guilt trip. As Chuck tells it:

We went into a bar and sat down. The bartender said, 'Who are you?' Don replied, 'I'm Don Stuart and I work for the Council of Churches.' The bartender asked, 'What do you want to drink?' Don answered, 'Scotch and water.' So the bartender brought the drink and

Don paid and left. The next night he went in again and the bartender said, 'Hi. You're okay. I called the Council of Churches and they told me what's up. You're welcome any time—and we have a group of kids who meet in the back—no alcohol served—it's called Pearls and it's a drop-in space to get these kids off the street. So maybe after midnight you'd like to come.' Don did. And the first night he found six or eight kids lined up to talk to him. I think it was the first encounter they had with anybody who seemed to care.

What skills did Don Stuart have to draw on? As famed newspaper columnist Herb Caen recounted in 1965, he arrived with a quick wit as well as pastoral experience. "The Night Minister was tackled by a husky panhandler. Reverend Stuart replied that he had no money. He was only trying to save souls, and sometimes heels."

What backup did the Night Minister have? He soon had Chuck Lewis, taking over for him on the streets one night a week. Then, when the Night Minister became more of a known presence on the street, it became clear that there was a need for a telephone line to take crisis phone calls. Crisis line volunteers were led by Joanne Chadwick, who has remained active in many valuable roles, including serving as Co-chair of our 50th Anniversary Committee. The first crisis line counselors acted to send the Night Minister to people in need who called in for help. Don Stuart needed to call in as well. This was before smart phones, before cell phones, even before beepers. The first Night Minister had to call in himself—from pay phones.

Nowadays Night Ministry continues to combine phone counseling with on-the-spot ministry. Current Night Minister Lyle Beckman is grateful for that organizational design. "Without knowing it, Don Stuart and the first Night Ministry volunteers were able to set the foundation and the tone for a ministry that would continue for 50 years and beyond," says Lyle, who now leads two Associate Night Ministers, Monique Ortiz and Thom Longino, and

Chuck Lewis (left) and Don Stuart walked out together for the very first time as the Night Ministry on November 1, 1964.

several assistants. "We still use videos showing Don Stuart in our training of Night Ministry and Crisis Line Counselors," Says Lyle. "He is thought of fondly as we share the Night Ministry story with congregations and other groups of people who partner with us in this ministry. And, there are those nights when I'm standing on a particular street corner, and I feel honored to be able to walk in his footsteps."

Kid on a Bus

Chuck Lewis recalls a compassionate encounter of Don Stuart's, one that could have ended badly for the first Night Minister:

> Don got into trouble once because he put a kid on a bus; paid his way to go back to a little town south of San Jose. The kid called his parents and asked them to meet him at the bus station. The parents had already reported him as an individual who had run away from home, so the boy was a status offender. So when the kid came off the bus, the

police were waiting for him and picked him up. Then they contacted the San Francisco police and told them that they should go see Don Stuart because he obviously had been involved with a minor. So the police called out at Don's. When they realized who he was, they said, 'We got this call and just wanted you to know this is what happened. We contacted you. That is all.' They turned around and walked away. But he could have been prosecuted.

Don Fox, the third Night Minister, says that on the streets, "Don was very gutsy and courageous. He once talked a man out of setting off an explosive device—the device ended up in the Bay."

Getting to know his predecessor, Don Fox says, "He struck me as a very intelligent and very wise man. He was very warm. You had no trouble feeling at ease with him right away. And he had a sense of humor that could defuse a situation." Pointing out a trait that made him unusually well suited for this job in the 1960s, Don says, "He was a straight guy but he didn't have the limitations that a lot of straight guys have on understanding and relating to gay people." His love of the job shone through their conversations, as Fox observes, "Obviously he had a powerful passion for what he was doing."

And Don Stuart made a vivid, lasting impression on the night people he ministered to. Don Fox discovered this the night he found himself "recognized" in an all-night coffee shop on Polk Street. A waitress mentioned his first name. Upon hearing the name "Don" and seeing a clerical collar, an elderly man in the coffee shop stood up, and approached Don Fox with a look of happy recognition. He said, "Oh my word, Don," and launched into a recital of the many conversations they had shared at the old Hofbrau restaurant on the corner of Turk and Mason streets. "I felt badly that I couldn't remember him," says Fox, "and then it struck me—he thought I was Don Stuart." Even though this encounter happened in the early 2000s and Don Stuart had retired in 1976, this elderly man warmly and vividly "remembered" Don

Stuart (albeit mistakenly) three decades later.

Lyle Beckman, the fourth Night Minister, underscores Don Stuart's lasting impression. "Still now, people come up to me to share their memories and impressions of Don Stuart," says Lyle. "Many were in their teens or twenties when they met him, yet they still remember his kind words and acts of compassion. Recently, a man told me that in the midst of suicidal ideas, Don stayed with him for hours. 'He wouldn't let me go off alone, and I am so grateful. He changed my life.'"

THE REV. CHARLES H. LEWIS 1976–1996

"I'm a little guy, probably about five-foot-eight and shrinking every day," quips the Rev. Chuck Lewis, pondering what drew him to ministry.

"I think I've always been interested in the underdog. As a kid, I found this little pug dog who was just terrified and would hardly come near me. Finally, I was able to more or less capture this little dog and bring him home. He just needed someone to be there." Captivating lost souls and just being there aptly indicates the essence of Chuck Lewis's enduring involvement with the Night Ministry.

Inside this "little guy" is a big heart, a resonant voice, and a compelling presence as well as big stature in the life and 50-year history of the Night Ministry. The second and longest-serving of the four directors, Chuck accompanied founder Don Stuart onto the streets on the very first night in 1964, acted as Stuart's assistant and back-up until 1976 when he moved up to full-time Night Minister, and retired after 19 years as director, serving a total of 31 active years on the streets. Then, in retirement, he returned as a dedicated volunteer. Now, at 83, Chuck contributes a grace note to the organization by writing thank you notes for current Director Lyle Beckman, and by lending his sage advice, energetic presence, and vital spirit in many other ways. He still presents choir boy good looks with clear smooth skin and bright blue eyes, under his shock of white hair.

Happily for the Night Ministry, Chuck was able to notice a change brewing for the Council of Churches, the ecumenical organization that originated the Night Ministry, and guide the Night Ministry to financial independence as its own California non-profit religious organization, before the Council went bankrupt in 1989.

It's not surprising to hear Chuck say, "While I was the Night Minister, Night Ministry was pretty much my life. It was enriched by all of the people who I met, whose lives touched mine." He reckons he made contact with 4,000 to 6,000 people a year, admitting to a concomitant downside: rarely did the opportunity present itself to find out what happened to the people who were helped.

First to Notice Change

When you are out on the streets nightly, says Chuck, you have a front row view of changes affecting the city and entering our culture. "Waves move across a city and the Night Ministry is impacted almost immediately by these changes," Chuck reveals. "I remember being in the Tenderloin in the late 1980s and '90s and all of a sudden I looked around and I said, 'Wow. This place has changed.' It was home to Asians and Vietnamese, but they weren't on the streets. I looked up and suddenly saw a doctor's office that was Vietnamese, a grocery store with Vietnamese food, Chinese restaurants. All of a sudden Asian hair dressers appeared. Everything was going Southeast Asian. And you realized that a big chunk of property in the Tenderloin had rapidly changed from what it was before."

Likewise, Chuck watched the Summer of Love unfold—in North Beach where he was stationed as a Lutheran minister for the North Beach Mission.

"Whenever social issues come to the forefront, they show up first of all on the streets of the city and not in the bedrooms," he says. "We were aware that kids were coming to the city before the city was aware of it." Living in North Beach in 1966, he noticed a number of people sleeping under the bushes and on the side of Telegraph Hill. A place called the Last Exit opened up on Broadway by two itinerant "so-called" clergy, who invited in all kinds of street kids to get a "supposedly" free meal. The kids decided to taunt the police by putting a big five-gallon jar of white stuff in the window which was meant to look like cocaine. Actually, it was flour. The police would come in and then get angry because it was only flour, not cocaine. Then, a young woman was raped in the basement. "Once that happened," he explains, "the police moved in and cracked down on the whole North Beach scene. Those people then moved out and about half of them went to the Haight Ashbury district and became the nucleus around which was formed the Summer of Love in 1967."

The AIDS Epidemic

A decade later, a more dramatic and lethal social phenomenon appeared. Here, again, the second Night Minister was in on the ground floor, and very much involved in the affected community. The gay community welcomed Night Ministers from the beginning, for their genuinely non-judgmental approach. Chuck also gained acceptance for his involvement in two groups: in 1964 he was an original member of the Council on Religion and the Homosexual that put on symposiums for professional people on what it was like to be part of the gay world; and he was on the original executive committee of a civic group called Citizens Alert that investigated police brutality and harassment in the city.

Nevertheless, one night Chuck felt the full force of the wave that would engulf the gay community, right in his face at closing time in a bar.

"Suddenly one of the bartenders came roaring out from around the bar, stared right at me, in the face, and yelled, 'Goddammit! What are you going to do about this AIDS crisis?'" he relates. "'I've got AIDS now and I'm going to die. And I want to know what are you doing about it?' Well, up until that point I hadn't really heard much about it because the first indications were only discovered and labeled about June of 1981 and this was now November."

It didn't take Chuck long to figure out how the Night Ministry could help. He immediately talked about AIDS with the crisis line counselors, helping to dispel any fears that the counselors, or their callers might have as to

PHOTO BY BRANT WARD

Chuck Lewis listening, as shown in the San Francisco Chronicle in 1984.

the method of transmission—it didn't happen by drinking out of the same glass or using the same doorknob as an infected person. More compellingly, Chuck decided to get an AIDS test himself to support people who were afraid to take the test. As he puts it, "So I could say here's what you do; this is what will happen; this will be anonymous; it's guaranteed. I took the test myself; nothing to worry about; go take it."

What You Deserved

More poignantly, the Night Ministry gave its precious presence to individuals affected by AIDS. "We also served as people ended up in the hospital," says Chuck, remembering when one of his assistant night ministers went to a hospital to visit a young man who was seriously ill and dying. The Night Minister asked the young man if he would like his parents to come and visit from Ohio. After much hesitation, because they had kicked him out of the house many years ago, the young man finally said yes. The parents came to the city. They got off the airplane. They came right to the hospital. The Night Minister was there in the room, Chuck says. The parents stood in the doorway and looked at their son and said something like, "Well, I guess you finally got what you deserved." And with that, Chuck says, they turned around and left the hospital and went back to Ohio.

"Fortunately the Night Minister was there and able to provide a different understanding for this young man," says Chuck. "That although even his own flesh and blood, his own parents had rejected him—totally—that the Night Minister didn't. And neither did God."

"I think the great message is not only that you are loved, but that you are lovable," says Chuck, broadening his observation to include most everyone whom the Night Ministry reaches. "Because most of the people we see don't really love themselves. And the message is that you are accepted and that you are not alone. And not only by the Night Minister but by some higher power in your life, that the Night Ministry may help you to get in touch with."

Hope, Community, and Continuity

"I think one of the things that the Night Ministry offers is a recovery of hope—a sense that life does not have to continue as it is. And a sense of giving me back my identity—not as people want me to conform in society, but an identity which belongs to me, which gives meaning to my life. Beyond that, I think the Night Ministry offers a sense of community because it helps people discover community where they are and not community where they think they ought to be. The Night Ministry goes out to where people are and helps them discover the community of which they're a part—and brings out the loving aspects of that community that make hope possible."

As society becomes more secular, will there still be a need for ministers? "I think the need for human compassion will always exist," Chuck says simply.

"Compassion for me means 'with passion.' That's the shape of the ministry. It means going with another person, even into the moment of their death, if necessary. That kind of ministry will never grow stale, and will always be needed. People can continue to exist in intolerable situations as long as they're not alone. As long as they feel that there is hope."

The motto of the Night Ministry, "Lighten the Darkness, Rekindle the Hope," came out of a discussion under Chuck's guidance to decide what the shape of this ministry should be. "I think that's one of the descriptions not only of the Night Ministry, but also of ministry wherever it really takes place," he says.

Chuck Lewis has lived out a call to lighten the darkness and rekindle the hope for nearly 50 years, in his astonishingly enduring ministry.

PHOTO BY BILL WASSON

A SUSTAINING MINISTRY

THE REV. DONALD A. FOX 1996–2007

"One of the powerful things about the Night Ministry that makes us a unique organization is that we offer opportunities for people who have a need or desire to pray but just don't have the opportunity," declares the Rev. Don Fox, the Episcopal priest who served as Night Minister in charge from mid-November 1995 until January 2007, overlapping both with his predecessor Chuck Lewis so he could learn from him, and with his successor Lyle Beckman so he could guide him.

Called to head the Night Ministry when he was 55, after heading pastoral ministry in Episcopal congregations, as well as teaching at the college level, Don has career experience and an administrative perspective that enables him to identify one of the key reasons why this ministry has survived for 50 years: the nature of the composition of the Governing Board. "Unlike any other church body that I've ever worked with, like vestries or parish councils, the Night Ministry Governing Board has avoided the kind of petty internal clashes and fights that go on in many church bodies," he observes. "Because the members have no hidden agendas and come from different denominations as well as different congregations, they serve only because they really care about this ministry."

The board focuses only on ministry and raising money to support it. "I think that is one of the remarkable things about the Night Ministry—and one reason it's been sustained for 50 years."

By the time Don started as Night Minister in charge, the Christian denominations that originally funded the Night Ministry had little by little reduced their grants. Registered as a 501(c)3 nonprofit in 1989, the Night Ministry came to rely increasingly on donations from individual congregations, individuals, community organizations, and the Governing Board's own fund-raising efforts.

Finding that the Assistant Night Ministers and Crisis Line Counselors were almost exclusively of Protestant background (plus one Greek Orthodox), Don worked hard to recruit Roman Catholics to make the staff more completely interdenominational. Roman Catholics joined the Board, too.

Aware that the Bay Area had become one of the places in the world where people of different major world religions were increasingly living side by side, and where Christianity and Judaism were no longer the only religious influences, Don wanted to ensure that the Night Ministry was positioned to remain effective in this new environment. The Night Ministers and Crisis Line Counselors had always served all persons regardless of their religion, or even if they had no religious affiliation—as well as regardless of their age, ethnicity, social or economic status, or sexual identity or orientation. But they themselves were of only Christian background.

In order to minister more effectively to persons of other religions, Don began suggesting to the Governing Board that it consider incorporating into the Ministry's staff and Board clergy and lay people of other religions, such as Judaism, Buddhism, Islam, and Hinduism.

The response of Board members was split: a third supported the proposal, a third wanted to stay Christian-centered, and a third didn't have a concrete position. The Board has since adopted a by-law allowing people of other religions to become members, and Don hopes that eventually both the staff and Board will become multi-faith.

Pending that change, the work of the ministry is enhanced by having clergy of other faiths available to respond to specific faith-based issues that clients may bring to our ministers or counselors.

Ideal Job

Don continues to be actively involved in the Night Ministry by ministering on the streets one night a month. Occasionally he steps in for Lyle, at his request, when a representative of the Night Ministry is needed at some community event. The work continues to be a source of fascination, joy and nourishment for this priest who in conversation is a tenacious questioner with an active curiosity and a broad interest in people.

"This job is ideal for me," he says, "because every night is an adventure. You really don't know what's going to happen."

Take, for instance, the time when he thought he was going to get slugged. This was in the days before cell phones, at a time when Night Ministers would respond to pages from Crisis Line Counselors by finding a pay phone and calling in to the office to find out who was in need of an in-person visit, and where to go. As Don was calling from a pay phone in response to such a page, he was aware that a man was coming up beside him. "You always have to keep aware—it's just common sense—to keep aware of what's going on around you, beside, behind, and in front of you," he says. So he knew that a tall, disheveled man with long hair was walking toward him. As he tells the story:

> I watched him out of the corner of my eye, while I was talking on the phone. And when I finished the call, I said, "Can I help you?"
>
> He started talking very pleasantly—he saw the collar. He was a Vietnam vet, he loved the church, and went to a Catholic school, loved the nuns. I guess he thought I was Roman Catholic. Then came the punch line. He wanted me to give him money. I explained to him our policy is to never give out money. We'll help in any other way we can. First, I didn't have any money, and secondly, we have to treat everybody the same. If someone on the street sees us giving money to one person, then he and many others could say, "How come you gave to her and not to me?" What would we say?

I told that to him. He just got mad because he wanted money and he cursed under his breath and stormed away. I had a second call to make, so I was back on the phone again, and he came back. But this time he didn't just stand there. Right in the middle of my call, he depressed the receiver and cut my call off. I said, "Why did you do that?" He said in a very low, angry voice, "Because you weren't paying me any attention." He began getting more and more agitated and louder and louder and cursing. Apparently he had come from some kind of fundamentalist Christian background because he could quote Bible scripture right and left. He was quoting scripture at me and saying, "You're no man of God. You're of the Devil."

He was getting closer and closer and his spittle was beginning to hit me in the face he was that close. And he was very, very angry and I was expecting a slug to come at any moment. I'm a non-physical kind of person. I didn't know what I was going to do. I wouldn't fight back and I was too scared to run. But I didn't want to look like I was scared. I was expecting a slug to come—when all of a sudden, two other guys—big, burly guys, bigger than he was—walked up and said, "We want to use the phone." So the guy yelling at me stopped and backed up and moved away a little bit. Then the new guy put his coin in and started talking as the first guy continued his tirade against me. Really loud. Finally the guy on the phone said to the first guy, "Will you shut up? I can't even hear!" And then the two of them got into an argument and they were really vicious and shouting at each other.

I decided this was my moment to escape. And I did. I walked very fast out of there. That was the closest I've come to being assaulted.

"The Church" and the Night Ministry: Common and Divergent Missions

Don thinks that "The Church" has much to offer to people who would never dream of darkening the door of a church. At the same time, members of many

Nocturnal Don Fox
engaging in his ideal job.

traditional "walled" churches misperceive people who live on the street. More complexity to the interrelatedness of "The Church" and its mission to carry out the Gospel comes from differing interpretations among Christian denominations of what it means to carry forth the words of Jesus. The Night Ministry finds itself at the crossroads in nearly every configuration.

"The Church has so much to offer, potentially, to people including those in dire straits," says Don, referring to Christianity in broadly general terms. "The Church" has a reputation, he opines, "usually deserved, of being judgmental and not being compassionate, not having the love of Jesus, so many people wouldn't dream of going to 'The Church' for help," he says—or even for spiritual fulfillment. "They've written off 'The Church' as hopeless." Many members of the gay, lesbian, bisexual, transgender community fall into this group.

"So here is the Night Ministry, representing "The Church" to literally thousands and thousands of people over the years who never have contact with a church. That's a really astonishing and uplifting thing," he says. "We do celebrations of life and marriages for people we'd never meet in church. They need prayer. But they're not welcome in church because they're gay or dirty or poor, or because they stink. Yet they want these things. So we do it for them, even outdoors if need be, or in a bar. I've had marriages and funerals in bars. They're just as meaningful as in a church."

Or, he simply dispenses prayer on demand. "We've all been asked many times in the street by total strangers, would you pray for me?" he says. "I always ask, 'Do you want to pray right now, here?' Sometimes we hold hands and pray right then in the street. The institutional Church is not able to provide prayer opportunities for people who don't go to church—especially in the middle of the night."

Conversely, Don has given many talks to parishes about the work of the Night Ministry, countering preconceived notions about street people. Don has often been asked if he was ever afraid. "These questions usually come from a church crowd when I give a talk—part of our education—to help these people be a little more compassionate by forgetting their illusions," says Don. "I say to people who ask me if I'm afraid of people who are dirty, homeless, or drunk, 'If you would forget what they look like and just engage in a conversation with them—just say hi, even just make eye contact—you will probably be astonished to find out that that person is enjoying meeting you.' It certainly is appreciated because most people don't bother to even say hello."

"One of the big differences between us and churches is that we in the Night Ministry are a hell of a lot more loving than most churches in the sense of really seeing people as equally valuable and equally lovable—whether they believe in Jesus or not. One of the big differences is that we are not evangelizing, not trying to convert people." But the reality of evangelism on the street and in your face offers a different kind of challenge to Don.

Striving for Non-Judgment

For Don Fox, the essence of Night Ministry work is being compassionate and non-judgmental in as all-inclusive a manner as possible. For him, the challenge is not accepting so-called undesirable people and refraining from judging those who many deem unlovable—the unwashed, the mentally ill, the angry. Rather, his challenge is in refraining from judging the evangelists who try to "save" people. "The worst challenge I can think of is encountering evangelical fundamentalists on the street who are out trying to convert people," he says. "And who want to get into an argument." These evangelists try to get people to change their way of life—to stop being gay, for instance. Meanwhile, Night Ministers are spreading a non-judgmental acceptance. "And then the evangelists get into an argument with us and tell us that we're going to go to hell," he relates, describing on-the-ground confrontations. Just thinking about it, he reveals, "My stomach is hurting because of the anger I have for these people. So I can hardly be non-judgmental with them." Admitting to his own inner struggle, he adds, "I'm judging those people and I just can't stop it and I shouldn't—but I am."

Nocturnal Temperament fits Ministering at Nighttime

The nighttime can also be peaceful, especially for natural creatures of the night—like Don. "We deal with people not only because they're in trouble, but also because they're night people who are most active and alert at night," he says, putting his finger on a little remarked, if innocuous, human distinction. "And I'm one of those people." This includes folks who like to work in the night shift, like coffee shop workers or bartenders. Ever mindful of the downtrodden, Don goes one step further. "We night people are the world's last unrecognized oppressed minority," he says, championing an unheralded oppressed minority. "We live in a culture that actively judges people who are active at night as people who have something wrong with them. We say, 'early to bed and early to rise makes a man healthy wealthy and wise.' Or, 'It's the early bird that catches the worm.' All of that is judgmental language against nocturnal people. When we work with night people, it's clear to them that we're not judging them. We recognize them as full-fledged human beings equal to daytime people."

What does his family think of his calling? My family, mostly Roman Catholic cousins, were very proud to have me doing the kind of work I was doing," says Don. "The others, I think, probably thought I was a little crazy. The Night Ministry became my family. It is where I put all my time and energy."

PHOTO BY THOMAS MIKKELSEN

THE REV. LYLE J. BECKMAN 2007–PRESENT

Born in Lincoln, Nebraska, and raised in St. Paul, Minnesota, the Rev. Lyle Beckman was mystified in the 1960s by news of violent anti-war demonstrations and insulated from encountering the likes of flower children. "I remember watching the news about San Francisco and the Summer of Love and thinking I don't really get all that," he says, recalling his days as a 16-year-old. "But in the back of my mind there was also some intrigue."

Prior to being ordained in the Lutheran Church, he says, "I pretty much thought I would end up in a small town congregation and live happily ever after." Instead, here he is in San Francisco, at age 62, living into a gritty, powerful ministry on the streets at night. He is also leading the Night Ministry into expansive new directions.

Don Fox hired Lyle as an Assistant Night Minister in 2004. "It was a very powerful and moving experience right from the beginning," says Lyle. He still loves being out on the streets at night, practicing "the Night Ministry saunter," a slow walk that invites eye contact and conversation from passersby. Sometimes the last person a street person wants to see is a priest, so their eyes dart away, or they just nod politely. "Since we all wear clerical collars, a lot of times people might just want to ask the generic questions about life," says Lyle. "Is there really a God? And if so how do you know? What is faith all about? What is life all about? I enjoy those conversations very much."

Sometimes just being present can be enough to make a difference. "We've had folks come up to us and say, 'I was just about to do something that I would have regretted,'" Says Lyle. "I think they're implying buying or selling or using drugs, or doing something that would have been illegal or hurtful or harmful to themselves. They see us and we don't even have to exchange a word, but it reminds them, wait, this is not the way I want to live my life. We also want to make sure that people understand that we're not representing a God that is angry, vengeful and judgmental, that we're representing a God that is compassionate, caring and forgiving, one that is able to help them heal and be built back up. That anyone can be transformed by God's love and by God's grace."

A deeply attentive listener, Lyle says he gains as much from the people he ministers to on the street as they might gain from him. Early in his time with Night Ministry, he was sauntering in the Tenderloin when a woman asked for prayer. As Lyle remembers, "I said I'd be delighted. I asked her name and did a pretty generic prayer, nothing spectacular. She told me as much. She said, 'I was thinking you would do something more like'—and she went into an incredibly powerful, long, pointed prayer. It was a good lesson for me. Now when people ask me for a prayer I usually give them options: do you want a simple churchy prayer or do you want a prayer from the bottom of my heart? That tells me a little bit more about them. I can pray from the bottom of my heart, but I give people the option now to be really just covered in prayer."

Shortest Tenure, Biggest Expansion

When Lyle started, the Night Ministry was an effective but small organization. There were just two activities—the crisis line telephone and Night Ministers on the streets. Don Fox, the third Night Minister, was the only full-time employee. An Assistant Night Minister would substitute when he was off, and Lyle became one of six fill-ins. A part-time office assistant started working in November of 2006, just before Don told Lyle of his impending retirement and asked him to apply for his job. When Lyle took over on January 1, 2007, the office assistant moved up to full-time. That was the beginning of a steady expansion of programs, personnel, and budget—and for Lyle, immersion

Lyle Beckman visiting with an old friend.

in bigger waves of administrative work on top of routine ministry and spokesman duties.

Lyle was supported from the beginning by Chuck Lewis, the Second Night Minister, who has volunteered for behind-the-scenes tasks and Don Fox, who serves as an Assistant Night Minister. Both have remained close for advice and counsel. The number of volunteer Crisis Line Counselors has remained fairly constant, fluctuating from 30 to 45.

The Governing Board supported the expansion, increasing the annual budget dramatically, from $150,000 to nearly $400,000. Much of the office space, event space, and parking space is donated by churches, or the budget would be much higher. Profits from invested reserves, not principal, have been tapped each year. "It's like so many of the miracles in scripture, there's always a little bit left for tomorrow," says Lyle, living out his faith. "We live by that. It puts our faith and trust in God's call of what we are doing and the community that supports us."

With a grant from a family foundation and support from Tom Robertson, then President of the Board, the Night Ministry started a two-year fellowship program. In 2008 Valerie McEntee, Monique Ortiz, and Diana Wheeler became the first three fellows, each working 20 hours a week. When Thom

Longino was hired as a full-time Assistant Night Minister, it meant that the Night Ministry could have four or five ministers on the streets on any given night. Open Cathedral, a daytime open air worship service, was launched in the same two-year period. "It was wonderful," says Lyle simply. "When I think back, it was a pretty exciting time."

Typical Day?

"There isn't one," says Lyle. Now that his role has expanded into that of Director, every day is different. "That's one of the reasons I like Night Ministry," he says. His typical 12-hour day starts mid-afternoon with meetings on Night Ministry matters or with community organizations that receive referrals. Or he will make a presentation to an agency like the San Francisco Mental Health Board; or talk to groups like the Lion's Club. No opportunity is missed to tell the Night Ministry story to interested people, including members of the press.

Lyle does paperwork in the evenings, and then attends another round of meetings or evening events for the Night Ministry, or partner organizations, or neighborhood groups like clergy serving the Tenderloin. Lyle keeps up with several collegial ecumenical groups and the Interfaith Council, even though they meet at 8:00 a.m. "That's an awful time for me," he confesses, because his

Offering care and compassion at Open Cathedral.

primary workday begins at 10:00 p.m. and doesn't end until 4:00 a.m. That's when he starts work with seminarians, field workers, Crisis Line Counselors— and also walks out to minister on the streets himself. "You want to know when I sleep?" he asks rhetorically. "Whenever I get the chance."

He just goes flat out from one task to the next, yet is always able to devote undistracted attention to the concerns of whomever he is speaking with, focusing completely on that person's needs.

"Sometimes I have to admit there are nights when I've done already maybe six hours of paperwork, meetings or other administrative things and it comes close to ten o'clock and I think, 'Oh, I don't know that I really want to go out on the streets tonight,'" confesses Lyle. "But as soon as I do, and I start having conversations, I am reminded that I love what I do. Every conversation that I have has some importance—hopefully to the person I'm talking to—but also to me. It reminds me that the work that Night Ministry does is valuable and it's an honor and a privilege to be a part of Night Ministry." Here are a couple of stories:

I was sitting at a bar one night and talking with a man who told me that he was suicidal. That always gets my attention. So I asked him to tell me what led up to him being in a bar and telling a Night Minister that he was suicidal. And so he went through this long story about his loneliness. And then we got talking about faith, talking about the fact that he was a New Testament scholar. That he had been angry with God. We talked about his need to control God and to control his own life and it turned out that this was an incredibly powerful conversation that he never thought he would ever have with anyone. And it was just as we kept going along, there were enough tags that made me hook onto a word or a phrase that helped him open up a whole new understanding of really what his issue was. And that was his issue of power and authority rather than an issue of having a series of bad relationships that he could blame on somebody else. So, after a long conversation—and we've kept in touch—he's doing much better.

I left the bar and the first thing I heard was a man looking at me and saying thank God you're here. Now, what's this going to be? It was a man who was schizophrenic, who was shooting at the aliens who were coming down to earth. We were being attacked. And so he thought that because I was a priest, I could, with my spiritual powers, help him to ward off this attack. So he and I stood on the corner of Polk Street and Sacramento and we shot our arrows at these aliens. And we defeated them. So San Francisco is safe because of our work that night. And then we sat down in a local coffee shop and had this incredibly powerful conversation about the kind of fears that he faced every day. And we were able to get him down from the aliens invading San Francisco to his fear of dying and his fear of dying alone. And then all of sudden in this very lucid moment, we talked about how he might create and sustain healthy relationships.

And I saw the two of them as being so alike in so many ways, even thought their lives were so different. Within two blocks of each other were two incredibly fascinating people who would have never talked to each other, but fortunately I was there to talk to and get them reconnected to life—and for each of them I think that's what happened—they were each more reconnected to life, and the larger world in a much healthier way.

The People We Serve

A great big, gentle, soft-spoken presence, Lyle stands as a steadfast advocate for the marginalized. "The people we serve are no different than you or me," says Lyle. "Sometimes when I preach a Night Ministry-themed sermon, I refer to the parable of the wheat and the tares, because it's so easy for us to judge. Quickly, we want to point our finger at the people who are offending us,

including people who are on the streets beg-
ging or being noisy. It's so easy for us to just
want to shove them away. In this particular
political time in our country, more and more
cities are making it illegal to be homeless, to
sleep in public or to be out there asking for
money. These are human beings. If you would
take the time to get to know them, you would
find (in most cases) someone who is sweet,
lovely, and wonderful, and also vulnerable,
afraid, maybe sick, really needs help, is so
tired because they haven't slept in months
and that's affecting their thinking and their
being. But they're human beings first. Deep

Preaching in the open air.

down inside there's always something that God can use to transform them.
There's always something we can say to remind them that they, too, are a child
of God like we are and that we have more in common than we don't."

A Gift of the Church and to the Church

Being non-judgmental is an incredibly powerful gift that ministry can give to
people. "To be able to meet people where they are, is incredibly powerful. At
Open Cathedral, people can come high or with a can of beer in their hand. It's
fine. It doesn't mean we condone illegal or illicit or unhealthy behavior, but
we don't have to fix everything all at once. We start by creating a relationship.
Do people change over time? Absolutely. We're responsible for a lot of people's
sobriety. We meet them at a time when they're able to hear a word that says
you must feel awful—tell me what it's like to be struggling with your addiction. When they hear themselves talk about what it's like to struggle with their
addiction, they're looking for help. We can offer them some help."

But Lyle wants to give something back to the broader Church which founded the Night Ministry. "I hope the Night Ministry has the opportunity to offer the Church a different approach to ministry," he says, referring to Night Ministry as a role model for the currently emerging Church. "Rather than expecting people to receive only what organized religions offer, we meet people where they are—literally—and figuratively, seeking to find out what they need and meeting those needs, thereby putting into practice basic tenets that underlie our common fundamental teachings. We practice loving our neighbors as ourselves through good hospitality, compassionate care, and radical acceptance. By supporting us in being 'the Church's night shift,' the Church has helped us to grow into a ministry that freely offers the word of love and grace."

Crisis Line Counselor listening on the phone.

THE SAN FRANCISCO NIGHT MINISTRY AT FIFTY

BY LYLE J. BECKMAN

T he San Francisco Night Ministry provides crisis intervention, counseling, referrals and pastoral care to anyone in any kind of distress, anxiety or difficulty from 10:00 p.m. to 4:00 a.m. every night of the year, as it has continuously since its inception in 1964. We do this primarily through the presence and efforts of our ordained Night Ministers who literally walk the streets of San Francisco and of our trained volunteer Crisis Line Counselors who answer telephone callers.

We are unique. We are the only San Francisco organization that provides person-to-person counseling and outreach in the middle of the night 365 nights a year. We have never missed a single shift in 50 years. There are other organizations that venture into the nighttime hours occasionally, but not every night. And we are the only organization anywhere that combines middle-of-the-night in-person help on the street with help over-the-phone every night.

When the Night Ministry began in 1964, we were one of only two organizations that had a crisis telephone line, the other being San Francisco Suicide Prevention. Fifty years later there are several, but the Night Ministry continues to be unique among them all in the San Francisco Bay Area. Some will talk with only certain people about certain issues; we are the only one that will talk to anyone about anything—there is no specialized group of persons or problems that we address. We are the only crisis line whose counselors can offer a face-to-face visit in matters of crisis intervention, by arranging for a Night Minister to meet with the caller.

In addition, we are the longest continuously operating Night Ministry in the country. While The Night Ministry in Chicago began in 1962, it ceased operation for a time in the mid-1960s.

And, we are unique also because we sponsor regular outdoor worship services that have a sacramental emphasis with weekly Eucharist (Holy Communion) and occasional baptisms, weddings, funerals and healing stations. Our two weekly outdoor worship services are each followed by a meal and a time for private conversation.

In addition, we offer complementary programs. We sponsor a gathering for Bible study and community building on Tuesday evenings. As part of our Wellness Program, registered nurses walk the streets with Night Ministers to offer basic first aid and health screenings, information, education, and referrals. The Night Ministry is also involved in a number of collaborations and partnerships with various organizations.

Recently we have added three additional programs. We sponsor the Annual Interfaith Memorial service for San Francisco's Homeless Dead each December; we operate a Van Ministry to more easily reach people in need; and we offer a Clinical Pastoral Education (CPE) Program for the training of seminarians and clergy.

We are sometimes referred to as "The Church's Night Shift" because of our valuable contribution to the ministries and programs of congregations and Church-related social ministry organizations that operate in San Francisco.

Night Ministers on the Streets

On November 1, 1964 the Rev. Donald Stuart and the Rev. Charles Lewis walked out onto the streets of San Francisco for the first time as "Night Ministry"—a project of the Department of Pastoral Services of the San Francisco Council of Churches. This walk followed a two-year pilot project modeled after The Night Ministry in Chicago and programs in Sydney, Australia, and London, England, to determine the need for such a program here. The pilot

The Revs. Monique Ortiz (center) and Diana Wheeler (right) ministering on the streets.

project also answered the National Council of Churches' question of whether congregations in San Francisco were responding to the needs of the growing numbers of youth who were arriving in the City seeking a new life, but finding life difficult here.

Night Ministers, all ordained clergy from a wide variety of Christian denominations, still walk the streets of San Francisco in neighborhoods where people are outside. They offer a listening ear, prayers and blessings, general information, and referrals to social services. Night Ministers also provide crisis intervention when needed. Often these walks lead them into bars, coffee shops, grocery stores, hotel lobbies, and other places where people gather in the night. Crisis agencies, including WOMAN Inc. and La Casa de las Madres, sometimes ask Night Ministers to provide transportation to "safe houses." Night Ministers also respond to callers to our crisis telephone line who request a face-to-face conversation.

In the years leading up to 2014 our three full-time and eight part-time Night Ministers engaged in an average of 18,000 substantive conversations each year.

Crisis Telephone Line

In 2014, the Night Ministry has 45 trained volunteers who serve as Crisis Line Counselors. They answer the phone each night of the year not knowing who is on the other end of the line, or the reason for his or her call. In a typical night callers face loneliness, isolation, grief or anger. Some struggle with relationships, jobs, or illness. Others deal with suicidal thoughts, depression or anxiety. The majority of our callers are women. Most are from the San Francisco Bay Area; however, a growing number of callers from other parts of the country are finding us. In each case the caller will find someone who is non-judgmental, compassionate, empathetic, and a patient listener. In a typical year our Crisis Telephone Line receives 7,000 calls.

Our Crisis Line Counselors come from many walks of life, bring varied

gifts and life experience, and represent many ages, ethnicities, social and economic statuses, sexual orientations and gender identities, and religious and spiritual identities. All are over 18 years of age and all receive 40 hours initial training and 20 to 40 hours of continuing education each year. What they have in common is a strong desire to serve others, and a compassionate heart.

Br. Jude Hill training a Crisis Line Counselor.

Of all the crisis lines operating in San Francisco, we are the only one whose counselors will talk to anyone about anything—there is no specialized group of persons or problems that we address. And we are the only one whose counselors can arrange a face-to-face conversation upon request.

Open Cathedral – Civic Center

Open Cathedral came into being to bridge the gap that people living on the streets felt between their discomfort at attending traditional walled churches, and their desire to attend and participate fully in worship. They asked the Night Ministry to provide a safe and friendly worship service for them. We looked at the success of a number of outdoor worship services across the country and knew we could respond positively. We also knew that this would create new opportunities for members of congregations to extend outreach by offering a meal and having meaningful individual conversations in the context of direct service.

For a short while in the late 1960s, the Night Ministry offered a worship service at 2:00 a.m., but numbers were too low to stay viable. So, on Easter Sunday, March 23, 2008, Open Cathedral – Civic Center was born. We gather each Sunday at 2:00 p.m. on public space near City Hall. This worship service includes praying and preaching, readings and singing, and a celebration of the Eucharist (Holy Communion). This is followed by a lunch donated by a congregation or civic organization, and time for the same pastoral care, counseling, and crisis intervention that is offered each night.

On average 75 people gather for worship and 150 lunches are distributed each Sunday.

Open Cathedral – Castro

As an outgrowth of a similar weekly outdoor worship service in the Castro neighborhood that was begun in November 2009 with moderate success, the Rev. Diana Wheeler helped to focus our efforts on partnering with other organizations and coordinating special events in that neighborhood. These include the distribution of ashes each Ash Wednesday, a procession of palms each Palm Sunday, caroling each Christmas Eve, and candlelight vigils to remember Harvey Milk, George Moscone and others who have died who are associated with the LGBTQ communities.

Open Cathedral – Castro is also a virtual community for more than 800 people. We maintain a page on Facebook and other social media sites, which offer inspirational stories, updates on events happening in the Castro neighborhood, and the opportunity to request prayers each week.

Open Cathedral – Mission

On May 19, 2011, our third Open Cathedral began. The Rev. Monique Ortiz was eager to duplicate the success of Open Cathedral – Civic Center, but this time as a bilingual English-Spanish worship service. Open Cathedral – Mission meets each Thursday at 5:30 p.m. outside the 16th Street and Mission BART station. We offer a meal and time for private conversation, prayer, and crisis intervention after each worship service. On average, 50 people gather for worship and 100 meals are distributed each Thursday.

At each Open Cathedral we meet people where they are in their own lives, invite them to participate at any level of comfort, and turn no one away. Our goal is to build communities that reflect the basic Christian values of love for one another and service to the world, while supporting and encouraging people on their own spiritual journeys. Attendance

Offering prayer in both English and Spanish.

Welcoming participation in Open Cathedral.

at worship is not required to receive a meal or private conversation, and often the busy outdoor marketplace settings expose the stark contrasts of life in the church and life in the world. While people are praying, singing, and reflecting on words being preached, they can also sometimes see acts of violence, abuse, and other realities of life on the city streets occurring nearby. Yet, each week faithful people gather together. Each Open Cathedral has been blessed by attracting an active usher corps—regular attendees who help set up for worship, greet people as they arrive, and supervise the meal serving; and faithful people who prepare and bring food to be shared. People who come from traditional walled churches are often moved by the experience they find. In their hospitality and serving, they become examples for us all.

Tuesday Night Gathering

Once Open Cathedral – Civic Center was well established, people began to ask for Bible study and other opportunities to get to know Night Ministry staff and other regular participants better. In April of 2011 our Tuesday Night Gathering began as a regular program of the Night Ministry. We meet on Tuesdays at

5:30 p.m. at the home of the Faithful Fools program in the Tenderloin neighborhood for a meal and time for study and conversation. Topics range from traditional Bible study to general conversations about faith and life. Limited to Open Cathedral participants, this program is building and sustaining strong relationships among people.

Wellness Program

In the course of walking the streets, Night Ministers find many people dealing with health and medical issues. Just as many people come to Open Cathedral because they are uncomfortable in traditional walled churches, so too, many of the same people don't seek medical care. So we started our Wellness Program, which pairs one of our volunteer registered nurses with a Night Minister on his or her nightly walk. These nurses offer basic first aid, blood pressure screening and sugar screenings, general health information, and referrals. This program provides a comfortable holistic balance by providing both physical and spiritual care at the same time.

Van Ministry

We have two vans augmenting our Wellness and Open Cathedral programs. To make our Wellness program more effective, the van offers a safe and private place for screening and conversation. It also allows us to more adequately distribute items donated to us, such as clothing, blankets, or toiletries, that make life on the streets easier to handle.

At Open Cathedral another van carries the necessary equipment for worship including tables, chairs, and sound system, as well as the food and other items needed for meal distribution.

Interfaith Memorial Service for San Francisco's Homeless Dead
Every December on a day close to the winter solstice, people all across the country gather to remember homeless people who have died that year. In San Francisco, this service was originally sponsored jointly by the San Francisco Network Ministries and the Coalition on Homelessness.

When Network Ministries ended its 40-year history of service to people in the Tenderloin neighborhood in 2013, we took responsibility for organizing and conducting this event, attended by 150 people, who gathered to pray, reflect, pay tribute, and remember those so easily forgotten.

SF CARES
SF CARES (San Francisco Compassion, Advocacy, Resilience, and Education Services) is a collaboration among four nonprofits: the Night Ministry, St. Paulus Lutheran Church, Grace Lutheran Church, and Welcome: A Communal Response to Poverty, formed to better close gaps in serving populations that all four groups share. We have feeding programs, educational programs, and other outreach efforts such as free vision screenings, harm reduction education, and domestic violence quantification. The collaboration started in November 2011 and offers a way for us to reach and serve people during the daytime whom we serve at night.

Interns and Field Workers
Since its inception, the Night Ministry has offered opportunities for seminarians and others preparing for ministry to join our programs to learn our model of ministry, which emphasizes listening and offers a non-judgmental, compassionate presence. These students come from the Bay Area seminaries

that comprise the Graduate Theological Union, the Episcopal School for Deacons, schools of social work, and chaplaincy institutes, often receiving academic credit for their time with us. Individuals have come from as far away as Europe.

Clinical Pastoral Education

The path to ordained ministry for many denominations requires at least one unit of Clinical Pastoral Education. CPE teaches the art of communicating with people who are in stress or conflict, are hurting, suffering, or needing someone who can be present with them, listen to them, and assist them in finding ways to solve problems. CPE helps caregivers to be less anxious with people in need or crisis. It teaches them to provide quality spiritual care.

Each unit involves 400 hours of learning both in the field, and in the classroom. Most CPE programs are situated in hospitals. We started this program partnering with Stanford University Hospital under their accreditation as members of ACPE, the national organization that gives CPE accreditation. Many seminarians seek an alternative site for CPE training; the Night Ministry is an ideal setting for this kind of learning.

Sacred Space – San Francisco

Sacred Space – San Francisco is a program for the city's LGBTQ community, providing a combination of pastoral care, counseling, and referrals, as well as a continuation of the special events initiated by the Night Ministry's Open Cathedral – Castro.

Two other groups contribute to this presence in the Castro: St. Aidan's Episcopal Church and Oasis California, an organization that is heir to The Parsonage, a 1977–87 pioneering program by gay people in the Episcopal Diocese of California to reconcile gay people and the Church. Sacred Space honors the 50-year-long commitment that the Night Ministry has made to ministering to the LGBTQ community.

Students of the Clinical Pastoral Education program learn the art of communicating with people who are suffering.

Other Collaborations

We cooperate with a number of other organizations on common goals. For example, we have an agreement with San Francisco Suicide Prevention to provide a framework to refer callers between our crisis lines, to cooperatively train volunteers, and to mutually support confidentiality and safety policies. We have an understanding with both WOMAN Inc. and La Casa de las Madres to provide safe transportation to a safe house for victims of domestic violence. In the wintertime, the San Francisco Interfaith Winter Shelter program provides overnight housing for homeless men; the Night Ministry sends a Night Minister to serve as an additional staffer at one of the locations, enabling an additional 40 men to be housed.

The Future

Often people will ask, "Will there ever be a time when the services of the Night Ministry will not be needed?" While our prayer is that all suffering disappear, and peace and joy reign for all of God's children, the reality is that people will always face difficult times, particularly at night. It is precisely for those who are in trouble, lonely, anxious, afraid, sick, or grieving at night that the Night Ministry was called into being, and why we continue our work today. We serve a valuable role as the Church's Night Shift, and have had a powerful impact on the lives of thousands of people each year.

We believe that our work helps to make San Francisco healthier, safer, and more stable for all who live and work here. We help to bridge the gap between the times when social services are available. We offer to build healthy life-affirming communities and neighborhoods. We offer companionship to the lonely and isolated. We attend to the mental and physical needs of those who are compromised. We provide harm reduction for those at risk to themselves and others. And we encounter and assist many of the most vulnerable who fall between the cracks, even among our city's very fine social services. All this is provided without receiving any public funds or charging for any services.

So, as we look into the future, what are our challenges and opportunities?

For 50 years, the Night Ministry has remained faithful to a simple mission statement: "Our aim is to help our neighbors in great need, when their needs will not be otherwise met in the nighttime hours."

Our approach remains compassionate and non-judgmental. As Roman Catholic priest and professor of pastoral theology Henri J.M. Nouwen espoused in his book, *A Spirituality of Caregiving*:

> Compassion is hard because it requires the inner disposition to go with others to the place where they are weak, vulnerable, lonely and broken. But that is not our spontaneous response to suffering. What we desire most is to do away with suffering by fleeing from it, or finding a quick cure for it.
>
> Yet, perhaps the greatest gift is an ability to enter into solidarity with those who suffer. Compassion can never coexist with judgment because judgment creates distance and distinction, which prevents us from really being with the other.

Baptizing a young soul at Open Cathedral.

While our purpose has changed little, and while the mild weather of the city continues to be conducive to our work, much has changed in San Francisco. From the beat generation, to the summer of love, to anti-war rallies, to a growing LGBTQ presence in the 1960s; through the AIDS crisis of the 1980s, earthquakes, economic ups and downs, the dot-com booms and busts; and with a growing population of people who struggle with poverty, homelessness and mental illness in the 2000s, San Francisco has seen many changes in culture, politics, economics, and population. One challenge will be to meet the needs of the people at night in a city that is always changing.

Another challenge for us is finding the resources to maintain and grow the ministry. In the early days we received funds that came directly from church bodies. When that stopped, congregations and individual contributors belonging to churches stepped in to support us. So for most of our history, our support has come from the Christian religious community. A few private foundations have sometimes given grants. We continue to sponsor fundraising events including galas, auctions, and concerts, featuring such performers as folk legend Joan Baez and jazz singer Wesla Whitfield. Other non-profit organizations make us a beneficiary.

Now, one of the great opportunities we have in the future is to continue to nurture that solid relationship with the Christian community but also to look for support from non-Christians, social organizations, foundations, and the corporate world.

We would love to grow the number of people we have on staff. From the early days of the Night Ministry through the early 2000s, on a typical night there would be one Night Minister and one Crisis Line Counselor on duty. Now, we draw from three full-time and eight part-time Night Ministers, and 45 Crisis Line Counselors. Simply put, if we can have more Night Ministers on the streets and more Crisis Line Counselors on the phones, we can serve more people each night.

Another challenge—can we move comfortably from being a Christian-based ministry to one that also includes representatives from the interfaith community who are not Christian? We will continue to seek to find ways to have a stronger interfaith presence in the future, without compromising our mission statement or changing our focus to be with those in need.

As we look to the future we want to continue to serve as a place for learning, providing field work and internship opportunities for students seeking a unique model for ministry and service. We would love to expand our Clinical Pastoral Education program, and will be open to enter into other partnerships and collaborations that will bring resources together from around the area to better serve the people of the night.

Mostly, we look to remain faithful to our calling to those whom we serve and for those who support us and send us out each night.

Lighten the Darkness, Rekindle the Hope
—San Francisco Night Ministry's Motto

465 POST STREET, SAN FRANCISCO 2   YUkon 2-4161

June 19, 1964

Rev. Donald E. Stuart
Trinity United Church
3900 Pace Boulevard
Lincoln, Nebraska

Dear Donald:

The Night Ministry Committee voted this morning
unamiously to extend you a call to become our Night Minister.

The call included an agreement that the salary will
be on the annual basis of $6,000 for 1964 with a review of the
salary position for 1965. The housing allowance has been
raised to $1,800 per year.

Acceptance of the call carries with it an agreement
to begin work no later than September 1, 1964.

Moving expenses will be covered up to $2,000. This
includes moving your household goods, your family transportation
to San Francisco and cost of temporary housing for your family
here while you locate your permanent housing.

The committee suggests you may want to come to San
Francisco about August 15th ahead of your household goods and
have those two weeks to search for your housing. It is possible
that Lewis Durham's house will be available for your use those
last two weeks in August, should you care to use it.

The matter of your health plan will need to be reviewed
with the United Church Conference here.

We await your decision with great interest and will
appreciate word from you at your earliest convenience. If you
have any further questions you would like to ask before making
your decision, please call me.

I trust you had pleasant trip back to Lincoln.

Cordially,

John Chester Smith
Executive Director

JCS:c

The letter that called the Rev. Don Stuart to be San Francisco's first Night Minister.

HISTORICAL HIGHLIGHTS

CONTRIBUTED BY CHUCK LEWIS, DON FOX AND LYLE BECKMAN

T hroughout five decades, the Night Ministry has continued to serve people in response to their needs. Their needs often arise in relation to events surrounding them. The following chronology of historical highlights places the Night Ministry's service in the context of some significant events that have taken place in the local community, the country, and the world at large. This charting of the Ministry's development from its earliest days, comes from the memories and archives of three Night Ministers: Chuck Lewis, Don Fox, and Lyle Beckman.

October 1962 to February 1963
A training and demonstration project is conducted by the San Francisco Council of Churches, the local interdenominational organization, for a potential ministry at night in San Francisco.

November 22, 1963: President John F. Kennedy assassinated

1963 to 1964
Funding is obtained for a three-year experiment from regional and/or national bodies (judicatories) of the American Baptist Churches of the West, The Episcopal Church, the Lutheran Church in America (now the ELCA), the Lutheran Church Missouri Synod, the Presbyterian Church USA, the United Church of Christ, and the United Methodist Church.

July 2, 1964: Civil Rights Act passes

June 19, 1964

The Night Ministry Committee of the San Francisco Council of Churches calls the Rev. Donald Stuart, United Church of Christ, to be the first Night Minister, with an annual salary of $6,000 and a housing allowance of $1,800.

November 1, 1964

The Rev. Donald Stuart and the Rev. Chuck Lewis, Lutheran Church in America, walk out together for the first time as the Night Ministry.

Responsibility for oversight of the Night Ministry is lodged within the Department of Pastoral Services of the San Francisco Council of Churches.

Telephone crisis hot line is housed in the offices of the Presbyterian Inner City Council.

First Assistant Night Ministers are hired and a volunteer Coordinator of Volunteers is named.

1964 to 1967

Service areas of the Night Ministry are coffee houses, bus depots, gay bars, young runaways, USO Vietnam War shows in the Tenderloin, and downtown.

Drugs of choice on the street are uppers and downers (pills) and marijuana.

1965: US sends troops to Vietnam

1967: Summer of Love in San Francisco

1967 to 1969

Service areas are coffee houses in the Haight Ashbury, gay bars, and among young runaways in the Polk Street corridor. Ministry continues in downtown, the Tenderloin, and the Polk Street corridor.

Drugs of choice are heroin, marijuana, amphetamines (speed), PCP, and hallucinogens (acid).

1968

The Night Ministry telephone crisis hotline is moved to First Congregational Church where it remains until 2004.

April 4, 1968: The Rev. Martin Luther King, Jr. assassinated

June 5, 1968: Sen. Robert F. Kennedy assassinated

1969

The Salvation Army begins to provide emergency housing for the Night Ministry at the YMCA Hotel.

> January 20, 1969: Richard M. Nixon becomes President

> July 20, 1969: Astronauts Neil Armstrong and Edwin Aldrin walk on the moon

> November 20, 1969: Occupation of Alcatraz Island by the group Indians of All Tribes

1969 to 1974

Service areas continue to be downtown, the Tenderloin, and the Polk Street corridor; the Haight-Ashbury is no longer a focus of ministry.

> April 2, 1970: First Earth Day

> 1970: Freedom Day Parade, first Gay Pride Parade in San Francisco

1971

The Night Minister is granted a three-month sabbatical.

> July 1, 1971: 26th Amendment allows voting at age 18

1972

A food pantry is begun at First Congregational Church for the Night Ministry.

> Summer 1972: Transamerica Pyramid, San Francisco's tallest skyscraper, is completed

> January 22, 1973: Roe v. Wade legalizes abortion in the US

1974

The 10th Anniversary celebration includes a concert by the San Francisco Chamber Orchestra and a banquet and worship service featuring William Stringfellow as preacher.

The YMCA Hotel makes free, emergency housing available to the Night Ministry.

> August 9, 1974: Richard M. Nixon resigns the US Presidency; Gerald Ford succeeds him

1974 to 1985

Service areas change. Coffee houses city-wide cease to exist. The USO closes. The Night Ministry extends its services to upper Market and Castro Street areas.

Drugs of choice become heroin and amphetamines.

1975

The Coordinator of Volunteers becomes a part-time paid position.

The Night Ministry Governing Board adopts a formal resolution confirming the procedures of the government of the Night Ministry in relation to the San Francisco Council of Churches.

April 30, 1975: The Vietnam War ends

1976

The Rev. Donald Stuart resigns as Night Minister after 12 years of service.

The Rev. Charles H. Lewis, Lutheran Church in America, is called as the Night Minister.

The Night Ministry hours of service are reduced from 10:00 p.m. – 6:00 a.m. to 10:00 p.m. – 4:00 a.m.

July 4, 1976: US Bicentennial

1977

Night Ministry salaries are frozen at 1976 levels through 1979.

November 18, 1978: Jonestown massacre at Jim Jones's Peoples Temple in Guyana

November 27, 1978: Mayor George Moscone and Supervisor Harvey Milk assassinated by Dan White

1979

The Ministry's 15th Anniversary celebration includes a worship service featuring the Rev. Eugene Boyle as preacher, and a banquet featuring Joan Baez as speaker and singer.

May 21, 1979: "White Night" riots following verdict against Dan White

1980

The Night Ministry begins its own financial accounting system and bank account, removing these functions from the San Francisco Council of Churches, prior to the Council declaring bankruptcy.

1980-90: San Francisco 49ers win Superbowls in 1982, '85, '89 and '90

1981

The Night Minister reports an estimated 1,000 homeless people sleeping on the streets in San Francisco. This is the beginning of a serious homeless problem for the city.

January 20, 1981: Ronald Reagan becomes President

June 5, 1981: Beginning of the AIDS crisis, with US Centers for Disease Control and Prevention report

1982

The Night Ministry is one of the first service providers in San Francisco to train its staff to relate to persons with AIDS.

The Night Ministry Governing Board adopts a permanent charter for the autonomous operation of the Night Ministry but is still responsible to and a part of the San Francisco Council of Churches.

1983

The estimate of homeless people in San Francisco increases to 5,000 and the City begins a modest housing program for them.

The Larkin Street Youth Center and the Diamond Street Youth Shelter open, with the assistance of the Night Ministry.

1984

The Ministry's 20th Anniversary celebration includes a worship service featuring Bishop Leontine T. C. Kelly, United Methodist Church, as preacher, and a banquet featuring Ruth Hastings and Co. The Anniversary Committee raises $20,000.

The Night Ministry telephone crisis line is moved to the church office within First Congregational Church. A new telephone system for the Night Ministry enables call forwarding and conference calls.

1985

The YMCA Hotel closes; the Night Ministry loses its emergency housing.

1985 to 1992

Service areas change. The Greyhound Bus Depot moves out of downtown. Ministry continues downtown, in the Tenderloin, the Polk Street corridor, upper Market Street, and the Castro Street areas.

The drug of choice becomes crack cocaine, resulting in a substantial increase in violence on the street and elsewhere.

The number of homeless people increases to 10,000.

1986

The Night Ministry experiences a decline in the number of volunteers to operate the crisis telephone line.

1987

A restricted fund is established to receive bequests from wills, memorials, and special events.

The San Francisco Council of Churches proposes a charter revision for the Night Ministry. The Night Ministry Governing Board appoints a Charter Review Committee to rewrite the Night Ministry charter, giving it more autonomy from the San Francisco Council of Churches. No further action is taken.

May 24, 1987: Golden Gate Bridge 50th Anniversary

June 1987: Start of NAMES Project AIDS Memorial Quilt

October 17, 1987: Loma Prieta 7.1 magnitude earthquake

October 19, 1987: Black Monday stock market crash

November 1987

The Rev. Lucy Kolin becomes the first female Assistant Night Minister.

1988

There is a dramatic increase in the number of AIDS clients and their families; both night and day services required by all concerned brings a new dimension to the work of the Night Ministry.

January 20, 1989: George H. W. Bush becomes US President

1989

The sponsorship of the Night Ministry is transferred from the San Francisco Council of Churches to the San Francisco/East Bay Urban Coalition.

The San Francisco Council of Churches declares bankruptcy.

June 20, 1989

The Governing Board adopts a charter establishing the Night Ministry as an independent organization and files as a 501(c)3 Nonprofit Religious Organization.

The Ministry's 25th Anniversary celebration includes a worship service featuring the Rev. Amos Brown, ABCW, as preacher, with music by Alice O'Sullivan and Dave Weber and the San Francisco Gay and Lesbian Chorus, and a banquet featuring entertainment by Ruth Hastings and Co.

November 9, 1989: Berlin Wall falls

1990s: Technology takes off with the Internet and personal computers

1990

The Internal Revenue Service and the California State Franchise Tax Board issue tax exempt status to the Night Ministry. The San Francisco/East Bay Urban Coalition sponsorship ends.

1991: Cold War ends with collapse of the Soviet Union

October 20, 1991: Oakland-Berkeley firestorm

February 28, 1991: Persian Gulf War

1992

Joanne Chadwick, Executive Director of the Commission for Women of the Evangelical Lutheran Church in America, offers her services to meet with executives from the original constituting denominations to plan for the future of the Night Ministry.

October 1995

The Night Ministry Governing Board holds a fund-raising benefit that later becomes an annual fundraiser. It features the Empress I José the Widow

Norton as master of ceremonies, and musical entertainment. About $8,000 is raised.

November 15, 1995

The Rev. Don Fox, an Episcopal priest, is hired to serve as the third Night Minister, succeeding the Rev. Chuck Lewis who is about to retire. Don accompanies Chuck on his nightly rounds to become more thoroughly acquainted with the Ministry's work.

January 10, 1996

The Rev. Chuck Lewis retires as The Night Minister. He volunteers to serve as the new Night Minister's "Secretary."

1996

A dwindling number of Crisis Line Counselors hits a low of four. The Governing Board considers dropping the crisis line because so few volunteers are answering calls. The Night Minister makes a case for keeping the crisis line as a crucial part of the Ministry. The Board agrees to his proposal to make a concerted effort to recruit and train more volunteers.

The Charles H. Lewis Special Service Award is established by the Governing Board to honor individuals for valuable services on behalf of the Night Ministry or the community at large.

February 1998

A part-time "Coordinator of Volunteers" is hired to handle the complex and time-consuming job of recruiting, training, supervising, nurturing, and scheduling Crisis Line Counselors.

March 1998

A newsletter is introduced, *The Nightly News*, "An occasional publication of the San Francisco Night Ministry." The editor is Board President Sherri Stieg. In her "President's Corner" article she points out that the Night Ministry has been San Francisco's only in-person crisis counseling service during the night for over 33 years, and that it is the United States' longest-running operation that offers emotional support and shelter referrals to homeless persons.

The number of Assistant Night Ministers fluctuates between four and six.

Night Ministers begin to use cell phones instead of pay phones. An initial donation of $250 and another of $570 by The Men of Grace, a men's group at Grace (Episcopal) Cathedral, buys the first cell phones and its contract.

October 1998
The fourth annual fall benefit, "Swingin' on a Star," features San Francisco Supervisor (and comedian) Tom Ammiano as master of ceremonies.

1998
The Board considers establishing a Foundation Fund, the goal of which is to achieve a principal investment that would definitely remain untouched, and which would generate spendable income. A goal is set to raise $500,000. However, following the advice of a potential donor, who asserted that, to be taken seriously, the Board needed to have a goal of at least $1,000,000, the Board raises the goal to that amount.

November 1998
The Governing Board formulates a mission statement, the first of three through 2002.

November 18, 1998 and January 20, 1999
In two Board meetings the Governing Board seeks to guarantee the ongoing financial support of the Ministry. With a bequest of $25,000 from Gordon Caven, long-time supporter and phone counselor for ten years (1985-1995), who died September 24, 1997, the Governing Board establishes a foundation fund (later named the San Francisco Night Ministry Foundation Fund). Pursuant to the Board's resolution, the money is deposited in an account separate from the general operating accounts. None of the principal of the bequest proceeds, or of the anticipated additional deposits to the account, may be withdrawn. The goal is to have the fund grow to the extent that eventually it will generate sufficient income to pay at least half of the Ministry's operating costs. A goal is set of raising $1,000,000. (Later more money originating from Mr. Caven's estate will be received, raising the amount in the Foundation Fund to over 47% of the $1,000,000 goal.)

1999

Unique contributions include:

Brad Perkins donates a computer, monitor, keyboard, printer, and scanner for the Night Minister's use, and two telephone headsets, a lamp, and a paper shredder for the use of Crisis Line Counselors. He also provides the Ministry with its first web page, recruiting Joe Stewart to design it.

A young Japanese girl from Kitakyushu, Japan, discovers a $5 bill lying on a beach in Hawaii. Unable to find the owner, she sends it as a donation to the Night Ministry.

December 1999: Coming millenium anxiety and Year 2K glitch fears

2000s: Technology makes email standard and mobile phones popular

October 7, 2000

The annual fall benefit, "Starlight Cabaret," features vocalist Wesla Whitfield and pianist Mike Greensill. A silent auction and a raffle are included. The goal: raise 15% of the Ministry's budget. Net receipts are $21,000, a substantial increase over previous fall benefits.

January 2001

Assistant Night Minister, Episcopal Franciscan friar Brother Jude Hill, SSF (Society of St. Francis) and Jungian analyst, is hired as the Coordinator of Crisis Line Counselors. He establishes a continuing education program, which is also available to the clergy who do duty as Night Ministers. He brings in professionals from various fields to share their expertise.

January 20, 2001: George W. Bush becomes President after
a sharply contested election

2001 – 2003

The Night Ministry moves its phone system and operation from First Congregational Church, which has provided space and utilities free of charge to the Ministry for 33 years, to a new location, which necessitates a change in the phone number. The new much larger space makes it possible to have more than one counselor on the phone at a time. It also becomes an office (replacing the "office" previously situated in the Night Minister's home). Storage space is also available. A new phone system is donated.

September 11, 2001: World Trade Center is attacked

March 15, 2003: US war against Iraq begins

August 2003
The Rev. Lyle Beckman begins work as an Assistant Night Minister.

2004
An economic downturn begins to reduce the Ministry's invested funds. Governing Board member Tom Robertson, who becomes President of the Board in 2005, takes a lead in the Board's effort to stop losses and ensure the preservation and growth of the Foundation Fund. The Board selects Petersen, Flynn, and Dinsmore to manage its investments.

November 21, 2004
At the 40th Anniversary celebratory Service of Thanksgiving at Grace Cathedral, participants include Night Ministers, Assistant Night Ministers, Crisis Line Counselors, Coordinators of Crisis Line Counselors, and Board members who had served since the Ministry's beginning; local leaders of the denominations that had been involved since its founding; and a choir composed of members of San Francisco churches that have supported the Ministry through prayer, contributions, and providing volunteers. At the reception following, the Rev. Don Stuart, Night Minister for the first 12 years, greets guests and signs copies of his recently-published book, *I'm Listening as Fast as I Can*. After sales of Don's book cover his printing costs, Don donates all of the future proceeds from sales of his book to the Ministry.

2005
The number of ordained clergy and life-professed religious serving as Assistant Night Ministers grows to a total of seven.

2006
Beverly Barrows, a long-time Crisis Line Counselor, is hired to work part-time as an administrative office assistant, and to do daytime follow-up, when

needed, to help persons whose needs were identified the night before.

Crisis Line Counselor and film student Deb Tullman, assisted by her cameraman Cortney Hamilton, produces a film to show the work of the Night Ministry, promote it, and also help train Crisis Line Counselors and Night Ministers.

April 2006
The practice begins of having two Night Ministers on duty three nights per week.

1996 to 2006
Service areas expand, serving 14 locations. The areas of the city covered by the Night Ministers vary, depending upon the need. The principle is to be present where people are at night, where they gather.

The intensity of the AIDS epidemic gradually decreases. Homelessness and the plight of many mentally ill on the streets keeps increasing. Estimates of homeless vary between 8,000 and 16,000 per night.

Issues of people calling the crisis line and encountered on the streets in bars, all-night coffee shops, or convenience stores include every conceivable problem. Records are kept of the most common issues in 34 categories.

Calls to the crisis line come from all over the Bay Area and beyond.

September 1, 2006
The Rev. Lyle J. Beckman begins full-time work at the Night Ministry.

Assistant Night Ministers earn $125 per night.

January 1, 2007
The Rev. Donald A. Fox retires and the Rev. Lyle J. Beckman of the Evangelical Lutheran Church in America becomes the fourth Night Minister.

2007: Start of Financial Crisis and Great Recession

March 23, 2008
The Night Ministry's Open Cathedral – Civic Center begins.

2008: Economic recession cuts social services; many non-profits close doors.

August 2008
The Night Ministry Fellowship Program begins.

> January 20, 2009: Barack Obama becomes the first African-American President

May 17, 2010
The Governing Board revises the charter to enable non-Christians to become members.

> August 4, 2010: Proposition 8 overturned in Federal Court; appeals begin

July 23, 2010
First annual Cabaret fundraiser for the Night Ministry is held at St. Aidan's Episcopal Church.

> November 1, 2010: San Francisco Giants win the World Series

> January 11, 2011: Ed Lee becomes the first Chinese-American mayor of a major US city

February 13, 2011
Local musicians present the first Spring Song concert fundraiser for the Night Ministry.

> 2012: Two-year-old Sit/Lie law, banning sitting or lying on sidewalks, enforced in the Haight and quickly spreads to other neighborhoods

> May 27, 2012: Golden Gate Bridge's 75th Anniversary

2013
The Night Ministry Wellness Program begins; trained nurses offer medical care to people on the streets.

Night Ministry assumes responsibility for the annual interfaith Memorial Service for San Francisco's Homeless Dead.

> 2013: Web 2.0 boom lifts San Francisco out of the financial crisis

> June 26, 2013: Same gender marriages, initiated by Mayor Gavin Newsom in 2004, become legal once again in California

February 15, 2014
The Night Ministry Clinical Pastoral Education program begins.

2014: Ellis Act evictions displace thousands of San Francisco residents.

2007–2014

Service areas continue to be the Tenderloin, downtown, the Polk Street and Van Ness corridor, Market Street, the Castro, the Mission, North Beach, the Third Street corridor, the Theater District, South of Market, Civic Center, and the Embarcadero.

Drugs of choice are marijuana and crack cocaine.

The areas of the city covered by the Night Ministers continue to vary, depending upon the need. The places that people gather shift from year to year, era to era. So the "beats" of the Night Ministers shift too, from year to year, era to era.

November 16, 2014

Grand festivities for the Night Ministry's 50th Anniversary include a Commemoration Service of Thanksgiving and a celebratory banquet with entertainment at Delancey Street restaurant.

APPENDIX

KEY TO AFFILIATIONS AND SYMBOLS

Denominations

AELC	Association of Evangelical Lutheran Churches
ABCW	American Baptist Churches of the West
ELCA	Evangelical Lutheran Church in America
JC	Jewish Congregation
LCA	Lutheran Church in America
LCMS	Lutheran Church – Missouri Synod
MCC	Metropolitan Community Church
NA	Not Affiliated
PCUSA	Presbyterian Church in the USA
RCC	Roman Catholic Church
SA	Salvation Army
TEC	The Episcopal Church
UCC	United Church of Christ
UMC	United Methodist Church
UPC	United Presbyterian Church in the USA

Symbols

* Member who has served as Governing Board President

† Member of the inaugural Board, then a 17-member subcommittee of the San Francisco Council of Churches

✦ Member of the present Governing Board

GOVERNING BOARD MEMBERS

COMPILED BY SUSAN STEVENS AND BRUCE PETTIT

This is a listing of Governing Board members who have served during the years 1964 to 2014. In the beginning, Board members came from one of the seven founding Protestant denominations. Later, they came primarily from donor congregations. In 2008, the Governing Board changed the Night Ministry's charter to discontinue Christian-only affiliation as a criterion for membership. Despite incomplete records, every effort was made to achieve accuracy.

Name	Denomination	Dates of Service
Ms. Barbara Allcox	LCA	1975-76
Hon. Fitz-Gerald Ames †	ABCW	1964-67
Ms. Barbara Anderson *	TEC	1988-94
Ms. Karen Anderson	LCA	1979-81
Ms. Kathryn Anderson	ELCA	2000
Mr. Ulysses Anderson, Jr.	MCC	1983-84
Rev. William Barcus	TEC	1986
Rev. Gary Berg	LCA	1972-73
Rev. Paul Berry	ABCW	1973-75
Rev. William Black †	LCA	1964-65
Mr. Embree Blackard	UPC	1983-84
Ms. Shirley Bohrer Capp	ELCA	2000-03
Rev. Stacy Boorn	ELCA	1988-90

Name	Denomination	Dates of Service
Ms. Marian Brischle ✦ ∗	TEC	2004-Present
Rev. James Clark Brown	UCC	1974-75
Mr. Joseph Brown	UPC	1969
Ms. Mary Parker Brunton	ABCW	1975-76
Mr. Fred Burdue	TEC	1979-83
Ms. Susan Burt	TEC	2004-08
Rev. A. J. Carter	UMC	1971
Ms. Carol Carter	PCUSA	1995-2001
Ms. Joanne Chadwick	LCA	1971-78
Rev. Marvin Chandler		1976-77
Mr. Buddy Tate Choy	UPC	1990-1996
Mr. Barry Clagett ✦	PCUSA	1999-Present
Rev. Dwight S. Coad	ABCW	1985-87
Rev. Clarence Colwell †	UCC	1964-67
Ms. Deborah Cote	ELCA	1999-2001
Ms. Grace Covington	TEC	1990
Rev. Michael Creighton	TEC	1971
Rev. Robert Cromey †	TEC	1964-65
Rev. Clifford Crummey	UMC	1966
Rev. Robert Current	UMC	1972-79
Mr. Larry Dannenberg ✦ ∗	ELCA	1990-Present
Capt. Stan Davey	SA	1967-76
Rev. Betty Davis	ABCW	1977-81
Mr. Philip Deemer	TEC	1977-78
Mr. Dennis Delman	TEC	1972-76
Mr. Paul Denning		1972-73
Rev. Kelly S. Denton-Borhaug	ELCA	1990-96
Rev. Brian Dickey	TEC	1982-84
Rev. Susanne Donahue-Bombosch	ELCA	1995

Name	Denomination	Dates of Service
Ms. Laura M. Dressel	RCC	1998-05
Rev. Jack F. Duffy	UPC	1970-74
Rev. Lewis Durham †	UMC	1964-65
Rev. Darrell Farnham	UCC	1972-79
Rev. Thomas Fattaruso	ABCW	1972-74
Dr. John T. Fazekas	UCC	1969-71
Ms. Rosalie S. Folger	ABCW	1987
Ms. Kate Fritz	TEC	1994-98
Rev. John Frykman	LCA	1979-84
Rev. John Gallagher	TEC	1969
Ms. Sheri Geesey	TEC	2002-04
Ms. Barbara R. Geisler	TEC	1979-80
Rev. William F. Geisler †	TEC	1964-65
Ms. Marilyn Geist	TEC	1982-83
Mr. Harold Gilbert	ABCW	1982-90
Ms. Ronny Gilmore	TEC	1976-77
Rev. Tom Gingerich	ABCW	1973-74
Rev. Wilfried E. Glabach	UCC	2005-09
Mr. Peter Goss	UCC	2008-09
Rev. William Grace †	UPC	1964-69
Rev. Victoria Gray	TEC	2009-11
Rev. Walter Grumm*	AELC	1975-85
Ms. Lois Guthrie		1993-94
Ms. Casey Hamel	RCC	2011-2013
Ms. Pam Hamel *	RCC	2002-09
Mr. Peter Hanson	ELCA	1991-92
Mr. Michael Haworth *	TEC	1987-90
Ms. Shawna Herschfield	ELCA	2012
Ms. Jennifer Hocking	TEC	2008-09

Name	Denomination	Dates of Service
Rev. Lynn Hodges	ABCW	1975-76
Ms. AnnaMarie Hoos	TEC	2005-06
Ms. Frances Horn †	UMC	1964-66
Mr. Timothy Huyler	ELCA	1987-2011
Ms. Ranae Hyer	ELCA	1984-89
Mr. Charles Jacobs ✦	ELCA	2007-Present
Mr. Greg Jahnke	ELCA	1995-99
Mr. Leland Jarnigin	TEC	1971
Ms. Susan Jeffries	UPC	1982-83
Ms. Kathy Johnson	ABCW	1976-77
Rev. Charles Kaldahl	LCA	1972-73
Rev. Stephan Kienberger	ELCA	1990-94
Mr. Ron King ✦ *	TEC	2011-Present
Rev. Hollinshead Knight	TEC	1969-71 & 80-82
Dr. Richard Koch	UPC	1969-71
Mr. Harold Kuhlman	ABCW	1972-79
Mr. Gordon Lahrson	ABCW	1976
Rev. Donneter Lane	ABCW	1977-82
Ms. Rosemary LaPuma	TEC	1994-95
Rev. Steven Larson	ELCA	1987-90
Mr. Lim P. Lee	UMC	1965-69
Dr. Elizabeth Lewis ✦	TEC	2010-Present
Mr. Ted Liebmann	MCC	1982
Mr. Roger Lindahl *	PCUSA	1988-03
Ms. Sharon Long	TEC	1977-78
Mr. G. William Lorton	TEC	1996-01
Ms. Joan Lucas	ELCA	1990
Mr. John Macdonald	RCC	2002-10
Mr. Harry Mack	UMC	1969-70

Name	Denomination	Dates of Service
Ms. Catherine Madison	RCC	2004
Ms. Snowden (Sandy) J. Manson	TEC	2005-07
Ms. Elaine Matthes	LCMS	1974-76
Ms. Valerie Mayer	TEC	2005-06
Rev. Ted McIlvenna	UMC	1965
Ms. Miki Meinke	LCA	1986-89
Rev. Ross Merkel	LCA	1984-85
Rev. Eric Metoyer ✦	TEC	2014-Present
Rev. Kenneth T. Miyake †	UMC	1964-66
Dr. Glen Molyneaux	LCMS	1965-72
Ms. Cathy Moreland	TEC	2010
Mr. Lester Morgan	UMC	1972-75
Mr. Roy Mosley ✦	UCC	2013-Present
Ms. Amy Ness *	ELCA	1992-93
Ms. Sue Nicholson	TEC	1984-85
Rev. Roy Nyren	UCC	1988-90
Mr. Jose-Manuel Pacheco	TEC	1996-05
Mr. Keith Packer	TEC	2010-13
Mr. Keith Parker	UCC	1985-86
Ms. Vera Parker	UCC	1985-87
Mr. David Peterson	MCC	1982-83
Ms. Mary Peterson	ELCA	1991-92
Br. Tikhon Pethoud ✦	TEC	2013-Present
Ms. Margaret Pettigrew	UMC	1967-69
Mr. Mike Phleger	RCC	2008-11
Br. Gilbert Pineiro	TEC	1992
Rev. M. S. Pinkston	ABCW	1971 & 1974
Mr. Philip R. Pollock	UPC	1984-87
Dr. John Prescott	TEC	2009-2010

Name	Denomination	Dates of Service
Rev. Walter Press	UCC	1965-72
Rev. Rob Rhudy	TEC	1978 & 98-2007
Rev. Jean Richardson	UPC	1988-90
Mr. Thomas A. Robertson *	TEC	2002-12
Ms. Jeanne S. Robinson	TEC	2008-09
Rev. David Rohrer	ELCA	2002-03
Rev. Rob Royall	TEC	1982-83 & 93-94
Mr. Jeremy Russell	NA	2007-08
Rev. Harry Schlitt	TEC	1976
Rev. Elmer Schmitt †	UMC	1964-70
Mr. Ron Schultz	ELCA	1990
Ms. Margaret Schuller	UCC	1968-82
Mr. William See	TEC	1965-66
Mr. Jake Shacklette	MCC	1977-78
Mr. Richard Shinn	LCA	1977-79
Rev. Ronald Shonk	LCA	1975-78
Rev. Douglas Siden †	ABCW	1964-72
Rev. John Chester Smith †	ABCW	1964-69
Major Les Sparks	SA	1976
Ms. Ginny Lewis Spiegel *	JC	2009-2013
Mr. Paul St. Francis	MCC	1977-78
Ms. Marilyn St. Germain-Hall	TEC	1992-2001 & 2008
Ms. Sherri Stieg *	ELCA	1994-2001
Mr. Frank Mel Studer	TEC	1967-71
Rev. James Sudbrock †	LCMS	1964-67
Mr. Arthur Sutherland †	UPC	1964-67
Rev. Harold Sutherland	ABCW	1980-87
Rev. Carl Sutter	LCA	1969-71
Ms. Marlo Tellschow	LCMS	1972-74

Name	Denomination	Dates of Service
Ms. Evelyn Thomas	ELCA	1996-2005
Rev. John Turpin	UPC	1971
Dr. Don Tusel	MCC	1979-82
Mr. Lauren Ustick	TEC	1983-84
Mr. Steve Van Landingham	TEC	1982-85
Ms. Mary Van Zomeren ✦	TEC	2012-Present
Ms. Ginny Wagener	LCA	1982-84
Rev. Hans-Ludwig Wagner †	LCA	1964-68 & 74-89
Ms. Kathryn Wagner ✦	ELCA	2012-Present
Mr. John Wahl	MCC	1974-89
Rev. Thomas Wajnert	LCMS	1981-82
Mr. Carl Wallis	LCMS	1967-74
Rev. Larry Walter	TEC	1990
Rev. Hugh Weaver	TEC	1967-69
Rev. John Weaver	TEC	1966
Ms. Edith K. Wells	TEC	2005-06
Mr. Herb Wells	PCUSA	1996-2002
Rev. Richard N. Wilmington*	TEC	1972-77
Mr. Ralph Winchell	UCC	1972-85
Mr. Roger Wolcott	TEC	1990-93
Mr. Gordon Yates †	UCC	1964
Mr. Ben Young †	UCC	1964-69
Mr. Richard Young		1971-72
Mrs. Ede Zollman	TEC	1991-2005